TRADEWINDS

Rea Rahaman

This publication contains the opinions and ideas of its author. It is intended to provide helpful and informative material on the subjects addressed in the publication. The author and publisher specifically disclaim all responsibility for any liability, loss or risk, personal or otherwise, which is incurred as a consequence, directly or indirectly, of the use and application of any of the contents of this book.

WORKBOOK PRESS LLC
187 E Warm Springs Rd,
Suite B285, Las Vegas, NV 89119, USA

Website: https://workbookpress.com/
Hotline: 1-888-818-4856
Email: admin@workbookpress.com

Ordering Information:
Quantity sales. Special discounts are available on quantity purchases by corporations, associations, and others.
For details, contact the publisher at the address above.

Library of Congress Control Number:

ISBN-13:   978-1-958176-78-8 (Paperback Version)
             978-1-958176-79-5 (Digital Version)

REV. DATE: 06/23/2022

By Rea Rahaman

Anger Control Management:

The Human Crisis

Substance Use Disorder & Addiction

Making Love

Juvenile Delinquency

Emotional Inquisition

Novels

Calypso George

Marine Moon

A Whole Lot of Trouble with a Little Bit of Hell

For my girlfriends:

Saleema Joseph-Ontario, Canada
Zorina Raghoobar-New Jersey, USA

Note from the Author

After writing four books on anger, I found myself reading romance novels. I read hundreds of them and realized that they were more of fantasy and drama, pain, and pleasure where the hero being male, who always has to save the female a victim in distress.

I found myself craving for more realistic adventure and less drama, where the characters are in a partnership, revealing true love and so Tradewinds was created.

I wrote with the intention that in the folds of these pages, both males and females will enjoy this story.

It's in honor of all counselors and law enforcement officers in the world who made a difference and contributed to people on Planet Earth. I have the pleasure of knowing some of them.

I hope everyone enjoys this story as much as I have had the pleasure of creating it.

Contact: rizefromanger@yahoo.com

Thank you.

Rea.

1

"Oh, what a beautiful day. I'm going to miss you."

The sun-kissed the clouds into whiteness leaving any darkness behind with the rain. The trade winds blew from the south through the palm trees, slowly swaying the branches from one side to the next, another beautiful, bright, sunny day on the little Caribbean island of Barbados. This little island stands alone from the rest of the chain of islands south toward the equator. Where heat shone from the sun, and where the trade winds blew its breeze to cool the inhabitants.

Slowly, the sun travels toward the west warming the Caribbean Sea. The reflection of the blue sky on the clear water gave the illusion that the water is blue. The smell coming from the sea was refreshing, as birds blow a mixture of different melodies with no special effects. The melodies enhanced the other sounds coming from the island which now forms a melody so sweet that it shifts everyone with romantic feelings. It is as natural and pure as the white sand on the beach.

No hurricane lay its eyes on the island this year however it did not stop the rain from pelting down two days ago, leaving a refreshing clean smell to the island, which the local Bajan people and the tourists alike love. It makes everyone feel clean and beautiful.

On the distant shores, waves create white ridges that crashed to foam on the rocks anchored deep below the sea. Along the horizon, a string of boats marked the verge of fishing grounds as fishermen returned with the night's catch.

On the other side of those shores, the natives are taking an early morning swim before the tourists evaded the beach for the day. Tourists of all color and creed from the world over traveled long hours, sometimes days to visit and enjoy the warmth of the islanders' culture and beaches.

This is an island with little crime, one of the lowest in the world, and the friendliest people on earth. The food is mainly from the sea, and the parties are a good mixture of socializing and fun. Nothing beats the Mount Gay rum and Coca-Cola or partying till the sun comes up from its night's rest.

The heritage of Africans lingered heavily in all corners of this 166 square mile island, outnumbering the British heritage, who were descendants of the slave masters. The slaves that inhabited this exotic island must have come from a peaceful African tribe because the natives always are happy. The smiles on the Bajans' faces as they go about their business for the day, the laughter in their conversations, and the good nature of their politeness are beyond what Maxwell Halifax had ever experienced.

"Oh, what a beautiful day," Maxwell repeated for the tenth time, which reality hit into his thoughts and interrupted the flow and he corrected his mantra. "Oh, what a beautiful day, yet so sad," Maxwell whispered to himself.

The early morning trade winds tussled with Maxwell's sun-bleached blond hair as he stood on the veranda, looking out at the Caribbean Sea. He is going to miss living here. He is going to miss the friendly faces, the beaches, swimming and surfing in the Caribbean Sea. This is the best part of his job. Traveling to exotic places, experiencing the natives and their culture is what he loves the best. It is nothing compared to a vacation, where the tourists' places are the main product. Tourists rarely experienced the natives and their culture; they missed out on so much.

No, that no longer works for him. Living among people who are not of your own culture is the ultimate experience in life. He was fortunate to have a job that provided this type of life. He was privileged to have experienced this in many countries. He loved his job and enjoyed every minute of it, however lonely he feels at the best of times. He's going to miss this country, where he had lived for the last two years.

Maxwell looked straight into the sea, as far as his eyes can travel, wondering what lies beyond the horizon. Who is smuggling what past the borders of Barbados through the Atlantic Ocean? Storms of various nature have been brewing for four years now, however this storm sure as hell is not a hurricane or pirates, it's a century-old drug smuggling storm.

Drug smugglers are the modern-day pirates of the Caribbean. Barbados is one of the main ports of transshipment for narcotics, which are bound for the United States of America and other countries.

Maxwell Halifax knew of the agreement between the United States and Barbados in connection with the drug trade that passed through its waters. These two countries signed a mutual legal assistance treaty (MLAT) along with an extradition treaty covering organized crime, conspiracy, and other common offenses.

Then in 1997 President Bill Clinton, Prime Minister Owen Arthur, and other Caribbean countries agreed and cooperated on the justice of counter-drug issues, along with trade development and finance. There's an Embassy of the United States of America in Barbados. There are about three thousand Americans that inhabit the island. Well, one less soon.

Maxwell looked to his left, seeing the boundary line of the island with its hotels and palm trees, feeling the cool sea breeze on his face and a sunburned nose. He had been living at this beach house owned by a police officer, Ian, who has been working with him on the present case since he arrived. They have become friends and Maxwell considered him his brother.

He took a deep breath and lazily turned his head to look for the last time on his right, where the beach stretched out beyond his sight. He inhaled and took a deep breath in and out as his eyes left the north ridge of the rocks, disappearing about a quarter of a mile into the blue waters, from the shore of St. Lawrence Gap.

His eyes traveled the length of the beach toward his apartment and then he spotted her. The hair on the nape of his neck prickled and he held his breath. His mouth dropped opened an inch as she walked along the beach with a blue and white batik wrap, tied around her waist, stopping high above her knees.

He forgot to breathe, too mesmerized and speechless as he watched her walk slowly without a care in the world coming into view in front of him. He inhaled deeply, taking in the sea air, the smell of the afternoon delight of sea and weeds. He loves this place, home away from home. Now, he loves it more.

What? She has turned around and is walking toward him. He glanced over his shoulder into the living room, off from the veranda. He is looking for his camera, spotting it on the bamboo tea table in the middle of the room. Damn! He looked back at the girl walking on the beach and glanced back at his camera. He had to make a decision. He did not want to make this decision.

Reluctantly, he hurryingly left his spot, ran toward the tea table, grabbed his camera, and set it into focus on her. He adjusted the zoom lens outward as he angled his camera, keeping a visual of her through the camera. He took a few shots of her, however, he desperately wanted a closer look. He waited and waited what seems ages nonetheless were only a few seconds as she walked closer. He was unconsciously holding his breath again.

The sun hit the lens as Maxwell angled his camera and it attracted her attention. He hit the go button. Ahh..... He got her. His heart tipped over with sweet gestures picking up a quick rhythm. He was pleased with himself for getting such a close-up shot. To his shocking eyes, something unbelievable took place, a surprise. He was mesmerized.

She stopped and turned her head, looking in the direction of the light that bounced off from something. Actually, it was the reflection of the sun's light that bounced off from something and caught her eyes. What can that be? The hair on the back of her neck rose, her instinct kicked in and her adrenaline shot right through her body.

She wondered with a frown. What could the sun's rays be bouncing off from? Then she saw him with his camera and felt his eyes upon her, looking. She felt their eyes connected for a split of a second before she realized that he had taken her photograph, bloody tourist now he captured her soul or so say the islanders.

What seems like hours, in reality, was only a few minutes, she stepped into his full frontal view. His finger touched the button on the camera and it clicked again, more pleased with himself than ever. He watched her disappear from his view. He left the veranda and ran towards her path. She was nowhere to be seen. He lost her. How is this possible? Where could she have gone? This isn't fair! He sighed. He gazed at his watch. It was time for the last day of work.

Tomorrow he would be back in Washington, D.C. in the United States of America.

In two hours, Maxwell climbed into Sargent Ian Blackwood's car heading into Bridgetown to the police department for debriefing and turning in the paperwork for the case that they had been working on.

"Mornin' man," Ian said.

Maxwell looked at his friend and stared at his smiling face then looked away. He is going to miss this happiness.

"Wa is wron' with ya, man?"

"Oh, I am going to miss you and this island," Maxwell said sadly. His eyes sweated tears as he looked straight ahead. Ian Blackwood turned left onto St. Lawrence Gap road.

"Com' bac' an' visit, man," Ian said, as he waved to an acquaintance waiting at the bus stop. On a regular day, he would have stopped and picked her up on his way to work as she worked down the street from his office however not today. It was a business day, and his friend is too sad to have company. Then he was going to have to explain Maxwell's sadness, which would be all over the island by sunset.

Ian knew he should be quiet and leave Maxwell to his thoughts. He turned the radio on as a calypso song tumbled through the speaker and he began to sing the song of a local calypsonian. It was a long half of and hour drive, the longest he had ever shared with Maxwell. As they climbed out of the car, he put his arm around his friend's shoulders and they walked with him into the police station toward the debriefing room.

Inspector Iniss Pentwood addressed the seated officers as they were seated. "Today, we sadly say goodbye to our friend Maxwell Halifax. We want you to know you are welcome hay anytim', man." Maxwell was too emotional to speak and nodded his head with a smile that carried his sadness.

"Ya man got it real bad," the sergeant said to Ian. "Now, to some pressing matters of de drug smuggling. Last night when everyone was partying up the hill, de boys and I went into Black Rock and we spoke to some druggies, who told us where to find our bad boy, Riad Kifer. We got the army to go with us and now he's all lac' up. Ah gonna break this ass soon and he goin' to talk. Halifax and I want to know who's the kingpin, the head nacho of de drug trade. We want de name."

Inspector Pentwood waited until the hailing and clapping settled down before he continued with his update. He loved this part of his job. "We decided to ship his ass back to Trinidad. We don't want no, no trouble with them Trini. Aah...got word from the top to send his brown ass back and stamp deportation on his pastpor'.

"He is so stoned right now and in a few hours, he will be in withdrawal, and then his brown ass gonna talk. Halifax going to get the name before he leaves. Officers get ya cell phone ready to get a photo of the drug lord in case he is here. I want proof. I want evidence, yo hea' man."

As the officers nodded in agreement he finished. "De army with two of yu is teckin' the trash to the airport at 2000 hours, when it's dark."

Inspector Pentwood looked at an officer and nodded to him. Sargent Malcolm Wagner turned to Maxwell and said, "Man, we got some good stuff fer ya." He walked two steps to Maxwell and put a folder on his desk.

He turned to the others and said, "Atta Halifax, ya gonna be brief on wha' a got out for the Trini so far. He got a wife and son who are under the constant protection of his bodyguards. His wife and son are in Longwood, Florida. The kid is going to a private school there and the drug lord is going to move there from where ever he hindin'. So where is he, we still don't know. Ah know man the name is all we want. Da comin" real soon. "

"Meetin' over, get back to wo'k," Sgt. Pentwood told the officers. He walked to Maxwell and he stood, shook his hand, and said, "it was a pleasure having you on our island. Ah neve' see a white man wo'k lik' ya. Ya com' bac' soon, ya hea' man." He turned and left the room as the other officers came and bid Maxwell Halifax goodbye. They all invited him for a drink after work at their usual hideout bar around the corner, down the street where Rita was already notified of the farewell party.

It was late in the afternoon when Maxwell stepped out onto the veranda a bit tipsy from the farewell party. The police officers who had helped Ian and him with the drug smuggling case left work at three in the afternoon heading for the little rum shop less than a mile in Bridgetown.

The owner, Rita, rushed them into the back of the garden where they drank 200-year-old rum shot and ate sugar cake, cornbread, and lots of other local delights. The food helped keep him from getting drunk, nonetheless, they were all tipsy. He lost count of how many of the single rum shots he had taken while the other officers took double shots.

A few hours later, Ian put him into a police car with a sober officer Peter Hicks and bid him farewell. No one was sadder than Maxwell. It was a memorable send-off, and one he will certainly treasure. Bags packed, he was now taking one he will certainly treasure. Bags packed, he was now taking in the last view from the veranda of the beach house.

He looked out at the beach and beyond the sea. His eyes scanned the sand searching for a female figure. He could not find what he was looking for, so his eyes rested on the view in front of him. He watched as the sunset on the horizon beyond the sea, his last sunset as the trade winds blew across the island.

As the sun made its daily journey in the west, the sky became a crimson color with golden clouds. The sea shunned the same color-changing swiftly as dusk approached. The last sun's rays now transformed the bright color into a dark wine hue, as it vanished into the faint shadow of the sea.

Working with the Barbados Coast Guard, Maxwell had spent many evenings aboard the Coast Guard boat when the sun went to sleep for the night, however, seeing one on land is different. The aftermath of the sun's rays glittered displaying hundreds of different colors upon the water, making it simmer with the delightful aroma of romance. He felt his loneliness.

Maxwell breathed deeply and walked to his bed, turned the lamp on, and viewed the photographs in the digital camera. He wished he could have met her. She disappeared as fast as she appeared. He fast-forwarded to the full-frontal view and let out a heavy breath with a husky laugh. He did really well, and he was proud of himself for the last shot of her. He couldn't see the color of her eyes or her face nevertheless it was good, heck it was more than good it was excellent.

He stared at the face that looked up at him, daring it to come alive. What a tan! Her face wasn't recognizable and he bet she had on no makeup. That is a first. It had been a while since he saw any woman without makeup except his sister. He gambled there was no eyeliner either, no lipstick, and no mascara on her lashes, a pure natural beauty. Where in the hell do you meet a natural beauty? Barbados, of course.

He is becoming silly, a grown man of thirty answering his questions and flipping his lid over a girl with no makeup. A girl, he thinks he has little chance of ever meeting. The thought made him feel lonelier as it began to creep into his heart.

Maxwell's eyes left her taunting eyes, traveling to the top of her head that carried her long black hair below her shoulders; he looked at her eyebrows down her long nose and back to her eyes. Well, where he figured they would be in person. Oh, how he wished he had captured her face more clearly. He looked at her lips and studied her parted lips then traveled to her eyes. What color are they, black?

An electric current exploded in his heart, hanging onto his spine. His eyes widened as he kept her in his gaze. He was transfixed. What are you telling me? What are you saying to me? He sat there for what seemed to be hours, however in reality only minutes, as he deeply breathes. His eyes continued their journey to her chin passing her red glowing cheeks down to her neck, down to her breast. Who cares if it is not how he imagined. He inhaled deep, looked at her blue bikini top, and back to the center where her breasts meet and climb a bit high. The bikini top outlined the center curves, tying at the back no doubt as he can only imagine where the straps disappeared.

Maxwell could not guess the size nor would he ever recognize her, even if she appeared in front of him now, dressed in regular clothing. He can definitely recognize her beachwear. Camera in hand, he went to greet the night. His eyes scanned the beach looking for her, reliving his brief moment of heaven. His last day and he had to see her. Two years in Barbados and this is what he gets, a natural beauty who came and went in the flash of a second, well in a few minutes.

Life's not fair. Maxwell left the beach house heading across the road, down the two stairs to the restaurant, for dinner. He needed more stairs so he can work off his sexual energy that now seems quickly to overcome his body. He is happy that he is wearing stretch shorts because he required the extra room. He cannot have people looking at him as if he is a sex maniac. The stairs did not help or the fact that he is a bit tipsy. He knows his arousal would be with him for a little while longer. He's glad that his t-shirt was out and not tucked into his shorts!

He found an empty corner table and sat down. He ordered a mauby drink, breadfruit, and flying fish stew. He was looking around at the restaurant when the waitress returned with his drink and said to him in her Bajan accent.

"Man, a se ya look so sad, ya leavin or somethin'."

"Yes, my flight is tomorrow morning. I am going to miss this place."

"Ahhh... se man com' bac' and v'sit, on holiday, not wo'k."

"I will and thank you."

As the waitress turned and left she said, "Ya welcom' man." He was sipping the drink, viewing yet again the photographs in his camera. He wondered if he will ever meet her, probably not, at least he had these photographs. How odd that the trade winds blew a natural beauty into his life, he thinks, therefore, he will call her his Tradewind.

As he tucked away from the local dish, his thoughts began making love to her on the beach. He sees them in his apartment in Washington, DC. He's going to have to release this sexual energy soon, real, real soon. For now, he will think of making love to her. His legs buckled, pulling her on top of him, as his backside hit the wooden floor. He felt no pain as she fell on top of him. Both laughing, he yanked at her hair as his lips found her partly opened ones, at the same time, rolling over her.

He stopped his thoughts long enough to pay his bill. He waved goodbye to the few regular people he knew at the restaurant as he took the stairs out to the night. He continued with his dream of making love to his Tradewinds as he walked to the beach house. He was on top; he entered her swiftly as his right hand firmly held her hips in place. Her legs automatically crossed over his back and she contracted, tightening her muscles, stretching her whole body.

The sound that came out from her mouth was music to his ear. Before either of them knew what was happening, they developed a rhythm that rocked their core, climaxing at the same time. She was honey and he was the bee!

Two hours later into the night of watching the photographs and dreaming Maxwell was ready to call it a night. As he climbed into bed naked, clutching his camera to his heart, he wondered whether she saw him, or was she looking at someone else. With the sun behind her high lightening her tan and beach costume, she looked sensational.

Sex appeal poured out of her core, filling the air with her aroma, he can smell it, feel it and he wanted to taste it too. Some women are fortunate to be born with classiness, which makes men fall over them. It is just his rotten luck that he does not meet any of them. How unfortunate that he had to see a sexy beauty on his last day here. He felt a perched sting stab his heart and he sighed depressingly. He needs his head examined. His loneliness swept into his heart; he closed his eyes and drifted off to sleep.

In the middle of the night, he saw himself standing on the edge of the same beach, outside his window. The sea breeze tossed his blonde hair from north to south, as he bumped into his sexy natural beauty, his Tradewinds. His fingers tips gently touched her shoulders, she turned and looked into his grey eyes, a smile lit up her face, and he held his breath. He pulled her back into his chest, his forehead met hers, his nose touched hers, he breathed in her aroma mixed with the midnight spray of the ocean, body to body blended into one.

They stood there for a long time before each started exploring the other body. Breathing heavily as their lips met, their hands left a warm sexual path of longing as they explored each other's curves. At first, his lips brushed hers and she laughed. Next, he let his lips lingered on hers, giving her a passionate kiss. Without further ado, his tongue darted into her mouth, making her breath freeze inside of her. One of his hands circled her waist, while the other was caught in her hair, holding her steady.

She felt the intoxicating brush of his lips and she was instantly aroused. An electric current zapped through her body, crossing over to him as their body melted into oneness. Sexual electricity went through her again inebriated with conquering the warmth from his mouth on hers. His hand pulled the bikini loose and she felt the wind on her breast. His mouth left hers, traveling to her neck then to the firmness of her breast. He took her nipple into his mouth and she buckled with a wild sweet sensation that ravished her senses.

Uncanny sounds came from her throat, making music to his ears; her bikini top was the first to go then the batik wrap was next and finally her bikini bottom, all lay on the sand along with his beach trunks. They were making love on the beach. He was lying beside her, his firm naked body close to her own, legs entwined, kissing, touching, and exploring. He moved them both in one smooth rhythm as she automatically moved her body to accommodate him. One hand cupped her backside and the other was mangled in her hair by her neck. He swiftly entered her and they climaxed together.

Maxwell was awakened and sat up in bed, wondering what just happened to him. It took a minute for him to gather his thoughts before he realized he was sitting in a pool of wetness. He had abandoned himself in the darkness of the night to a betrayal that left the sheet sticky. Darn wet dreams.

This is what he gets for thinking about the sexual release soon. He never had wet dreams before nevertheless the tension was gone. He laid his head on the pillow and closed his eyes thinking of her. He had a myriad of new scars to allocate to others collected over the years from the rejections of lovers. It didn't stop the few words that drifted into his thoughts on the wonder woman that he saw that afternoon.

My eyes are closed, oh how I think of you

My heart is racing and it calls out to you, my love

My breaths are quick because I dream of you

Once again, he fell into a deep sleep. Much to his disappointment, he didn't dream of the mystery lady again.

Maxwell's Tradewind awoke the very minute he did, shivering in sweet sexual body mist. She knew he had taken her photograph and he was dreaming about her. She had the same dream; she knew it was of the stranger. What is he doing dreaming of her? Why is he making love to her in his dream?

The myth about tourists taking the natives' photographs without permission was not a joke. The legend goes that the person in the photograph will haunt you. All her life she heard stories of peoples' spirits blending with a simple photograph as thoughts and heart became one as they collided with feelings. She never once believed any of it, until now. The myth became a reality. This means he is attracted to her and wanted her.

A male that thinks with his heart, a very rare occurrence and now she will never see him again. She pondered on it for a minute wondering as she laid her head on the pillow what would become of them. Would they meet? What is the possibility that they would actually meet? Would either of them know? Her thoughts drifted to the moment she realized that someone was watching her.

When she caught the reflection of the sun's light on the camera in her eyes, their spirits collided and now he dreams of her and she is receiving it. He evokes the essence in her body, apt and ready to be explored. Now they are together for the rest of their life, or until he gets rid of the photograph, bloody tourist!

One and a half years later, Maxwell was once again packing his bags. The case that he has been working on in Barbados and Washington, DC is now in Longwood, Central

Florida. It has been a long five years of investigating and collecting evidence, hoping to close the case once and for all. The drug lord has been living there for the last six weeks.

Although his wife and son were there, he was not present. He finally moved with a full twenty-four hours security detail. In the meantime, Maxwell was assisting other agents with their case while waiting for the drug lord to surface.

DEA agents in Seminole County had his family under surveillance. Today, Maxwell was given orders to close the case and find the evidence that would put the drug lord in prison. This would kill the drug trade in fourteen countries, at least for a while until another drug lord takes his place.

He is exhausted from all of the travelings and yearns to settle in one place with one hot sexy lady. It has been a long time since he was involved with anyone. Since he returned from Barbados he had a few one-night stands, only to release his sexual energy.

Each of the four women he had sex with had the face of his Tradewinds. He knew it wasn't fair on them however he let them know that there was no attachment. Guilt surfaced and he buried it somewhere, wherever emotions are buried.

Maybe he will get his wish. Maybe he will find someone in Florida who will quench his sexual thirst. Maybe he will finally settle with an exotic lady who will understand him and his job. Loneliness is what remains far and wide on him. He can taste it on his lips and feel it in his bones. This wanted fugitive of a drug lord bought a house in Longwood and his son is going to a private school there. Even a vagabond like him has a family. Some men have all the luck.

Maxwell made the call to the DEA office in Lake Mary to let them know he is on his journey there. The next call was to his roommate. He would be sharing a house with a police officer who lived in the vicinity of the drug lord. Meeting the drug lord and arresting him for having a business of illegal drug trade, spanning North and South America, even Europe is one thing. This is easy, however, having the evidence stand strong in court is a whole different matter. The justice system seems to be made to have some silly technicality set the drug lord free.

Europe wasn't his business only the United States of America. He has most of the evidence collected; nonetheless, he needed direct proof of the drug lord's connection to illegal drugs. This would be the final straw to light the bond fire on a drug lord and remove him from society. He's tired of the case and just wants it over so he can move on to something new and hopefully exciting!

Anyone coming forward and testifying in the Justice system would be good for his case, which will eventually seal the drug lord's fate in prison for the rest of his life. He can't wait and hope soon that he can have the connection. It is long overdue. When he put this case to rest he is taking a nice long vacation. He had accumulated a good three months of vacation time. Maybe he will go visit his family in Montana. With the drug lord operation out of business, he would ask for a desk job and maybe he too would find a nice sexy girl somewhere soon and settle in one place.

Unknown to both of them Maxwell and his Tradewind, serendipity had moved in and now pulled the spirit of their lives into full throttle, all from a moment of spontaneity. The energy of the Laws of Attraction is so unique woven into their lives the chances of them living life separately is nil to zilch. Is there such a thing, nil to zilch? Then again, the energy of synchronicity is there to lead a helping hand to the energy of serendipity.

It was after lunch two hours into the afternoon when the decision was made. She sat in court as the prosecutor asked her question after question. She answered and finally, he told the court no further questions. As she stepped down and took her seat behind her client's, she let her breath out. The lawyer for the defense of her client spoke however she did not hear a word. Yasmeen was ready for a glass of wine. It was a long winter; she needed dinner and a break from this case. She was happy it was finally over.

Testifying for the state to take control and release her fourteen-year-old male client from his mother was not so hard. Accepting the fact that a parent was abusive was the difficult part and painful. After months of counseling, her client pulled through his difficulty and was willing to go to a home in another county and live with a loving family.

The teen turned and smiled at her and mouthed a "thank you." Yasmeen leaned forward and touched his shoulders, giving him a tired wary smile. They won. She gave a final wave as she climbed into her car. The next three dozen cases await her attention. They will have to wait a bit longer, first things first, a massage, drink, and dinner.

2

Yasmeen was sitting in the British pub making notes from the papers she read. Next to her lies her Black and Tan. Maxwell was looking at her totally transfixed. He studied her from the top of her head to her waist because the bottom part of her body disappeared under the table.

There was enough to look at where he was sitting. The rest of her will come at a later time. He is thinking about what methods, yes method because he's sure that it will take more than one to seduce her. The seduction, his seduction has to have a backup plan, maybe more than usual. This lady is unusual from the rest of the common pack.

Maxwell rubbed his chin with his fingers as he continued to study her. Her short black hair sat wavy with short curls here and there, falling over her face and covering her left eye. Black is the color of her eye, he guessed. Her nose stood straight and long with wide red lips matching her red turtleneck cotton sweater. Her breasts rise well above the table, neither small nor large, medium built, enough to fill his hands. His body reacted to his vision and suddenly felt a motion as sensations revved in his stomach. His manhood extended and stood erect.

Damn it, he's so happy, he is sitting. He took a long sip from his beer. It hit him in the right spot cooling him down a bit, well not his manhood. The sensations did not even slam to a halt, which he was hoping for at least some control. He swears that his manhood stood more erect. The darn thing took a life of its own. Get a grip, you hard-up old fool.

Maxwell's eyes becoming a laser beam zoomed in for a detailed outline of her face. He observed her serious frown as she read off the papers in front of her. He can feel her essence calling at him. Yes, right, his left brain confronted the right brain.

She has warmth and a polished sexiness, which he found appealing. He can feel her internal strength and integrity. He liked her more now as he drew his opinion from her physical structure. He felt a reaction coming from his heart, warmth that he has not felt since he saw his trade wind in Barbados. Maxwell slightly touched his heart with his trembling fingers. Sweet breadfruit, please help him.

He couldn't understand why he was responding to her like this, like a magnet, as if he met her before, knew her all his life. If he had met her he would have known, he would have remembered. He doesn't ever forget someone as beautiful and as sensual as her.

Oh, hell bells, her energy is pulling him towards her. Oh hell, his is pure ....pure what? He cannot think, what was he thinking? Nothing, all he is feeling is intense emotions towards a lady that is sitting a few feet from him, pulling him into her parlor of sexual warmth.

Without warning, she lifted her head and their eyes collided the same as the morning breeze drifted off into the Caribbean Sea, touching his skin. She smiled and held his puzzled gaze for what seemed as if it were hours.

The few minutes their eyes connected, sexual sensations surged and traveled the short distance from one to the other evoking an intensity that killed time. Unknowingly, he automatically returned her smile. She smiled with her eyes giving him no choice, he followed suit. He was lost in her smile, in heaven. He let out a sigh with heavy feelings of relief and decided to chase the smile.

Summoned by her smile, he stirred finally. He pulled his entire body of his five feet ten inches, one hundred and sixty pounds of muscles on his feet. For once in his life, he was the richest man alive. Automatically he took his mug of beer with him. Ignoring his friends, he joined her, their eyes still locked together. He was as lost in her as she was in him.

Three pairs of eyes followed him and settled on her. One of his friends gulped his beer, the other choked on his pot pie and the other was left with his mouth opened. They knew that this was something special and understand that their colleague was about to step into the love zone. They looked at each other and grinned. All eyes turned back to the pair observing every movement. A few others' eyes also were observing them, stayed to be a witness as to what's to come.

Maxwell commanded her eyes to stay connected to his, as he walked lazily with his drink in hand and offloaded his mass structure of frame into the chair next to hers. Both eyes still linked, sending and receiving sexual sensations that fused the air into an electrifying moment of pure bliss.

The cold air in the pub became warm. Now, this fused with the warmth between them filtered with electricity, heating them to the maximum. Waves of pleasure cascaded through them generating intensified emotions. Knots of butterflies in their stomachs quicken their heartbeat. The stutter of electrifying sensations intertwined with several emotions rolling through their bodies.

Body temperature rose and vibrated in flushed cheeks with a soft pink color. Surrender was not wired into their systems, however, as they looked into each other eyes it became the first of the many control systems to be dissolved.

Anyone who looked and a few did see the electrifying surge of sexual sensations running from one to the other and back again, slowly building into something emotional. They continued to gaze into each others' eyes, unlocking more warmth, becoming speechless of the unspoken first moment of love, yet to be uncovered.

The waitress, Ava was on her way to deliver dinner and upon seeing the moment of true love stood still awaiting a time when it would be appropriate to intervene. She shifted from one leg to the next watching with his three friends and others all mesmerized with the impact of energy that sailed between these two soon-to-be lovers. She counted to ten and decided it is now or the food would be ruined. Ava arrived with fish and chips, resting them next to the papers on the table.

"Sorry it took so long, Yaz," Ava apologized. The food was on time however she felt she needed to say something and that was the only thing that surfaced through her thoughts.

Yasmeen reluctantly left Maxwell's gaze and smiled a thank you to Ava. She returned to him as he also smiled at the waitress with a no thank you to her question of ordering a meal. Instead, he ordered another beer.

Ss Ava left, his eyes returned to hers. Upon not being able to link their eyes together he watched as she pushed some papers neatly into a folder. He looked at the folder and noticed that it was marked confidential and then it disappeared under the table.

She then picked up her plate, rested it in front of her. He figured she is a lawyer, however, she doesn't fit the profile; what does he know. At this time all he knew was that there was something between them that he wanted to explore more. He watched as she poured ketchup on her fries, picked one up, and put it into her mouth.

Lucky fires, he thinks, wishing it was him. The thought clogged his lung and he found he could not breathe. He felt a motion react in his jeans. He gulped and took a sip of beer. It did not do anything. She went for the fish next and cut a piece off with her knife and fork, dipped it into a white sauce, and added it to her mouth.

No words were whispered between them. The silence was understood. Maxwell's eyes were pregnant with thoughts that he refused to express. He watched her as she slowly devoured her food, not once giving him any attention. He admired her for her appetite. It shows her passion for something else, he is hoping, later. He was grinning as his thoughts went to the latter with him bringing her to an orgasm as the main course and her breast for his nightcap.

She took a sip of her drink, licked her lips, and dabbed the napkin over them, wiping what she thinks she might have missed with her tongue. The licking of her lips took him over the edge, there was now motion within his ocean, they wanted out!

She looked at him. "Are you happy? Did you enjoy watching me eat? Is this a hobby of yours or somethin'?" The words came out from her as an angry cannon shot. He was speechless.

As he tried to gain control, he found breathless. His jaw opened to express himself and the words failed to relieve themselves. He lost control. Does she not know what she just did? This is illegal. She needs to be arrested. Their eyes once more linked. She looked at his opened mouth and put her hand up in the air, moving it from right to left saying very softly more of a whispering sound.

"Hello, Mars to Earth, are you there? Come in, Mars to Earth." The sound of her voice teased his thoughts for identification and he finally said, "Mars to Venus."

"What?" Yasmeen frowned in wonderment.

"Mars to Venus, you know men are from Mars and women are from Venus."

Shaking her head from right to left, "and obviously you believe it. That's stupid. No wonder the divorce rate is so high. We both are from earth unless, of course, people are marrying for everything else except love, which gives me permission to draw de conclusion that they don't know what love is?"

His lazy smile reached her heart and he replied. "I know how to love. I did learn a few things from that book. Do you want to know what it is?"

She smiles and said. "I bet you do. How's it working for you? How come you're still single?" Her elbows resting on the tables and her hands folded together supporting her chin. "Good for you, no, I don't want to know.

"Why not?"

"Because I am never concerned what with you know or what you have learned or from where. What I want to know and I am more concerned with is, what are your differences, how you work with those differences, and what you don't know," she informed him in her very slight accent.

Maxwell opened his mouth to object, instead, he took a breath and closed it, realizing he recognized the accent. It is not as deep as the natives of Barbados nevertheless it is there in certain words. He was about to ask her to validate his assumptions however he doesn't have the heart to change the subject. He can listen to her for the rest of his life, for all he cares!

"It's never what you know, it's always what you don't know. It's not how long you know someone only how well you know that person. It's not the quantity of something, only the quality of everything, mostly conversation, and relationships. To top that don't forget to stick some fun into it." Her eyes become flirtatiously wicked. Sexual sensations danced in her black eyes. A few minutes passed and the words fell out from him. "I am Maxwell."

"No kidding and those are your buddies you deserted over there," tipping her head slightly into their direction.

"Ah, they will survive." His eyes not leaving hers he added, "What is your name?"

"Now, I need Ava. I am ready to go. Oh! I don't have one."

"You don't have a name? He mused.

"Oh, I do. I am not telling you. You can find me a name and I will be that." She told him in a low flirtatious whispering voice that blows the air out of him.

"What?"

Men, she thinks, they are so boring, and they don't know how to play. They have to be spoken to in general terms and take the initiative in how to direct the path of the conversation. Otherwise, boredom takes over and all is lost.

As for American men, they have a chip on their shoulders along with the feeling of an inferiority complex. They are not trained to be gentlemen and respect has to be earned. How silly is this, earned respect. Never would that happen with her. Not working for any bloody respect. Mars is an understatement from where this species came from and they are not from Earth or Mars!

Somehow, she sensed that this male species' smile is different and he is not like the pack of men out there. There is something different and very sexy about him. She knows he is nervous and hopes that he doesn't know she is too.

Oh, how her lips ached to kiss him, her fingers itched to touch the contours of his body, to feel the pulse of his erection in her hand. With these thoughts, her cheeks glow a deeper color. She broke the link and removed her eyes from his hoping he did not see the rise of color in her. She looked at her empty plate.

Maxwell noticed the high rise of color upon her cheeks. He swallowed hard and felt a reaction in these tight jeans. This is the very last time he is wearing tight jeans. He is going for stretched ones. No tighter or fitted jeans for him stretched it is from this moment onwards. He was floored that she is responding to him.

Good, he has an effect on her. Maybe he will see her again. No sex tonight or one-night stands here. The thought of not seeing her again crept in somehow and he forces it out as fast as it came. Fear mingled with anger in his thoughts. Oh no, he has to see her again!

Ava returned and Yasmeen asked for her bill. She removed her hand that was supporting her chin and reached for her purse. Holding her wallet in her left hand out of his sight she looked at him. "Play, Maxwell. Quit being so serious, it doesn't look good on you." Those words spoken from her lips fired his senses into chaotic emotions. He processed them quickly and as meaning took over, warmth surfaced followed by affection. Play, he can, and play he will. He likes that, he thinks. Somehow unknowingly the chaotic emotions unknowingly turned to love.

Ava returned and put the bill in front of her. No sooner did it touch the surface of the table, Maxwell retrieved it. He reached for this wallet and pulled out some bills, covering twenty percent tip, and put it in the folder. He stood up, looked at her, and noted her shocked and surprised expression fused. He ordered, "Let's go." Her mouth opened again. Damn, he's going to have to do something about that!

Yasmeen sat there stunned, lost for words. She could not think. This is a first and with a total stranger, though he does not feel as if he is a total stranger. Has she met him before? He feels familiar somehow. She breathed out and took a deep breath again, knowing he is watching and waiting patiently on her. The world must be coming to an end!

She didn't know how to process this, except she likes the fact that he took charge. Her senses as well as her instinct are the best judge of anyone's character. She pulled it out from hiding to assess him before making any decision. Yes, she likes it when males take charge, not controlling or attentive, only to be in charge. Attentive men are boring and possessive.

A male taking charge is someone who knows not to cross the boundary line between them even after sex. He has integrity and respect. She does not care about him paying the bill as she can do that herself. Nice touch, nonetheless he possessed. What would it be like to have him possess her!

Get your thoughts out of the sex bin, girlfriend. She lingered in his order and warmth suddenly sprung up at his words. Hundreds of unknown cravings are awakened in her heart that she thought she had under lock and key. Her eyes never left his; she took another deep breath. She was trying to gain some understanding and control of her sexuality that's overtaken her thoughts and body. Too late, he made her lose it.

She took another breath as quivering responses touched her. A hand reached over and extended it to hers. She looked at the hand in front of her, her hands automatically reached and rested into his, as if it belonged there. She felt herself moistened and trembled. Sweet flying fish, her body is betraying her!

On the touch of hers, he trembled and his manhood twitched and roared more to life. It wants action. It requires action to cool down. Not tonight buddy, you are on your own, Maxwell telepathically informed his anatomy.

Yasmeen looked up at him frazzled from thinking, from feeling, and met his eyes. She slowly picked up her things, retrieves her keys, and began to walk with him. With his free hand, he waved to the waitress and said to his friends, "See ya."

Four eyes followed them out the door. All of them hoped the new acquaintances would be getting some loving tonight. They wished they could've had that connection with someone. Some people have all the luck. Maxwell pulled her through the door and let go of her hands. She stopped, disappointment written in her expression. His hand was warm and gave her comfort. She felt safe. She turned and bumped into him. His right hand touched her on her back, just below where her bra lies, laying there. She took a deep breath and asked. "You didn't want to hear what your friends have to say?"

He took the keys from her hands and replied. "No, I know what they would say, thank you. Where's your car?"

"Your friends would tease you, huh? My car is there, the back one." She points to the Jaguar sports car a few feet in front of her. He guided her the short distance and touched the button on the key ring.

"You have a Jag? In a world of Bens?" He sounded and looked puzzled.

"What?" Certain despaired. He challenged her to have the courage to glare at him in confusion.

"A man thing, forget I said it." Maxwell opened the door and let her through. He opened her hands and laid the keys in them.

"Thank you, that was thoughtful." She laid her handbag and case on the seat, turned, and faced him again. "Surprisingly and funny, I don't want this to end." She informed him with sadness in her voice.

Maxwell looked into her eyes and had a funny feeling she was feeling the very same as he was, neither of them wants the night to come to a halt. So he'll see her again, will he? His right brain said to his left and hurry, will you? A smile lit his eyes and he asked. "Do you want to go for a walk?"

"Yes," A smile shun in her eyes. "I know where."

The unity between grey and black eyes reached a point of no return. They traveled in a land of pure white light as they experienced comic love, unknown to both of them. The intensifying electric feelings that surge between them collided and for a split-second, time stood still.

Yasmeen mentioned to Maxwell where Crane's Roost Park was located and agreed that he would follow her there. He nodded and headed for his car. He glanced back and waved with a huge smile on his lips that touched his heart and reached hers too. He watched her climb into her car and drive off. He climbed into his and followed her, keeping a close distance.

Yasmeen drove fast, deliberately ignoring the speed limit. He happily trailed smoothly as she kept eye contact in her rearview mirror. She laughed and waved at him. They both arrived within a minute of each other and parked close however in different spots. She waited for him as he joined her. She took a deep long breath.

"You know, following me so close is illegal. You could be arrested for that driving," she told him humorously.

"I am so sorry. I didn't mean to scare you. I didn't know where you were going. Honest, I just moved here and have never been here before. I am mostly in Longwood." Then on second thought, he voiced, "You couldn't have gotten a ticket."

She laughed and asked, "Your car has a GPS service, why didn't you use it?"

She saw his eyebrow raised in surprise and he replied. "I like following you."

She shook her pretty head in disbelief and started to walk.

He followed taking the place beside her, her footsteps measured to address his as Maxwell recognized this, he let his long steps matched her small ones. They merged into a steady walk that entailed a good workout.

"I have a name for you."

She glanced at the new moon, stopped, and looked at him, saying, "That took you a while, what is it?"

He said, "Tradewinds."

"What?" Yasmeen stopped walking and looked at him in bewilderment. Baffled as to why someone would call her Tradewinds.

"You know Trade winds, the Trade winds of the Caribbean, the ones that blow the winds from the high-pressure area to the low-pressure area, across from Africa into the Caribbean."

"Seriously? I know what Trade Winds are, why Trade Winds?" She resumed walking and he followed.

"You are from the Caribbean, Barbados and you represent the wind that sailed into my life, trading my warm blood to hot." Like if in hells bells he knows why. The truth is, he doesn't know why nor does he understand why he said it. It sounds silly, then again, the minute he laid his eyes on her, he felt silly, compelled to be with her.

Maxwell wondered if he was trying to create his fantasy of the girl on the beach with his beauty standing next to him. She looks nothing like her. Then why does he want her to be his beach beauty? A strange emotion crept into him, one he never experienced before until now. He swallowed and breathed deeply, very deeply.

Silence took hold of them both for a few minutes as they maneuvered their path on the boardwalk. They tried not to bump into the other people that lined the rails watching the marine life that surfaced now and again. The bread was being fed to them as well as the birds and ducks that were the daily habitat.

The laughter came from her heart. "That's the sexiest thing a guy ever told me." Not, silly yes, corny, yes, sexy hell no.

"You know my accent?"

"I don't believe you."

"Mmmm, don't."

"That was stupid, wasn't it?" Maxwell had to ask.

She stopped walking and looked into his grey eyes. "No, not stupid, mmmm corny." She could not tell him the truth. She does not want the evening to ever end.

"You're Law Enforcement, aren't you?" Yasmeen asked him as they resumed walking the second lap around the lake.

He knew he doesn't want to lie to her. He knows that she is different from the other women he dated. He has plans for her, not tonight nevertheless soon, real soon. He cannot fend off his sexual desire for long. What plans and how far he wanted to take it, he didn't know. What he does know is that he does not want this night to end nor does he want to leave her. He looked straight ahead and replied with a "yes."

He added. "I am undercover law enforcement from the Drug Enforcement Administration, a DEA agent. There isn't much that I can share with you." He looked at her for any disappointment. He found none and breathes a silent breath of relief.

"That's okay," she replied. "There's not much I can share with you either, I am a counselor." As if reading each other's thoughts, they stopped, turned, and looked at the other. They silently understood their position. Confidentiality is a high priority, without a doubt. They resumed walking in silence for a few more minutes enjoying the moment of sharing and breathing. He ripped the silence by asking. "What music do you like?'

She was so involved in her thoughts she jumped, looked at him, and smiled. "Bob Marley, Queen, Journey, and Pink Floyd."

"Quite a combination, all foreign, none local."

"Blues, Journey. I am a vegetarian, only seafood?" She volunteered.

"Rock n' roll for me. I am all meat, potatoes, and barbeque ribs with beer."

"Wine." On second thoughts, she added for fun. "I know, it shows on you, you wear it well. I like the fact that you don't have a six-pack or an earring, you can't carry either. They will overpower you." She turned and grinned at him.

His face was covered in shock. He flushed and asked, "you check me out, when?"

"Of course, I checked you out, when you were walking toward me a minute ago. You have a problem with that? You were doing it to me the minute I sat down at the pub and when I couldn't take it anymore I looked up. How bloody rude!"

"Yasmeen, I have a tattoo."

She held her breath and smiled so wide that he held his breath. "I like tattoos."

They stopped for a few seconds and looked at each other then burst into laughter. As they resumed walking, he said. "Do you come here often?"

"Yes, every day," she replied.

"It's good exercise."

"Do you mind if I join you about sixish?"

"Is that in the morning or afternoon?"

"Afternoon."

"Mmmm let me think?" She deliberately allowed a few minutes to pass before she answered. "Oh well, guess your company is not that awful. The distance around the lake is one mile and I do four miles. I walk right to left."

"What?" He looked puzzled.

"Patronized Americans walk left to right, some are open-minded enough to walk the other way, right to left. Look around, some walk this way and the others that way." Pointing a finger in either direction as his eyes followed the finger and not the direction. Maxwell's thoughts wandered towards what he can do with the finger or what his fingers can do to her. Damn, this is trouble, breathe you silly fool, breathe.

They both had stopped and looked at the flow of human

traffic, walking in both directions. "This is my walk so we do it my way, when we do somethin' on your territory, we do it how you want it." She resumed walking and picked up the last few spaces turning towards parking. Maxwell momentarily gained some sort of control lengthen his step and followed her out of the boardwalk.

"We're here," she announced, turned, and walked in the direction of her car. Rejoicing that he would be seeing her again, more so that she wanted to see him again, he was beyond excited. He felt some action within him and realized that his motion wanted to sink into her ocean. His heart was dancing with laughter.

He plucked the keys out of her hand and opened the car's door for her, holding the keys for her to take. She turned to face him and took the keys. She leaned towards him, blushed as she put her hand on his chest, which encountered his damp t-shirt and she moistened.

She lifted her big black eyes and met his grey ones. She went on tiptoes and kissed on his cheeks. "Yasmeen Khan, thank you for the walk, I enjoy your company and I will see you tomorrow right here at six." She turned around, climbed into her car, and drove off. Looking through the rear-view mirror she saw his surprise fused with a shocked expression.

A huge smile highlighted her eyes sending a wave of sensation through her heart. She watched as his fingers touched his cheeks where she kissed him. She whispered ever so softly, 'I like him. Maxwell, I like you lots," and felt a surge of emotions run through her entire body. She inhaled and kept those feelings.

In heat of the night, in an endless moment of intensifying energy, she felt his presence. She turned and looked into his grey eyes just before his lips covered hers. She felt his kisses, soft and tender, teasing hers. His hands held hers behind her back, anchoring her in place as he deepened his kisses.

The pressure of his mouth spoke of his hidden passion and forgotten desires. She could feel his thirst for her rising from deep within him as his kisses became firm and filled with a hunger for her.

The whispering of sensations instantly awakened long-forgotten delights within her passion. Shivers of hunger swept through their hearts as her trembling lips fell apart and he entered her with his tongue, once again tasting her harmony.

His hand released hers and instantly she slid her arms around his neck, pulling him closer. One hand went around her waist, drawing her firmly against him. She molded her body to his and felt it melt against his, hungry for his touch.

The other hand pushed beneath her t-shirt, sliding it upward along with her bra then tossed it on the floor. Her breast fell naked and eager for his mouth. His fingers squeezed her nipple with a wicked precision as he took the other into his mouth. She struggled for breath and music left her throat as her hands unbuttoned his jeans. His body slightly moved away from hers, giving her easy access, cooperating with her, as she undressed him.

She pulled his jeans down. With rapid movements, he took it off along with his black underpants. She moved up and slid his t-shirt off. He took her white shorts off, followed with her underpants, all in a heap on the floor, joining the other clothes.

The joined venture of removing clothes completed, he scooped her into his arms as she giggled, both breathing quickly and unsteadily. Emotions run wild through their senses, devouring them. She bucked to him as he laid beside her with his naked body entwined in hers. Their hearts sang a song of love, as his warm lips nuzzled against the crook of her neck.

Is this love they are feeling? He moved and in one swift heartbeat, his prized possession entered her. His motion was sinking into her ocean. She cried out in pure delightful pleasure, whispering his name.

Maxwell and Yasmeen both awaken with a smile on their faces, both of them were having the same sensuous dream. He whispered her name and she whispered his, at the same time touching her lips. He felt her calling him, he felt her whisper his name, smiled and tightened his hold on her in his dream. He buried his face into the pillow as he was astonishingly overjoyed that the wet dreams stopped of the girl in the photographs he had taken so long ago in Barbados.

He was over the moon that his dreams are real and filled with a lady he met his afternoon. He wondered if she dreamed of him too. Funny, how their lives budded in reality and continued in a dream as if it was meant to happen. Can their dream become reality? He wondered whether what they have together is strong enough to withstand any trade winds. He hopes Yasmeen feels that whatever transpired between them this evening was worth sorting through and hopes it develops into something lasting.

She opened her eyes and realized where she was and whose arms were holding her close. He is definitely not the stranger who took her photograph so long ago on the beach in Barbados. The turn of events that led to this moment is beyond her comprehension. She was thrilled that the nightmare of the Barbados stranger was over. This person whose arms held her was the stranger she met that afternoon!

3

In the days that followed, Maxwell and Yasmeen walked and talked-talked about everything under the moon and sun, never asking questions, never talking about anything personal or professional, always exchanging information, laughing at the corny jokes, touching a little here and a little there, mostly laughing. They look forward to the moment of seeing and enjoying each other's company. The four miles around the lake became five then, six.

Silent moments wrapped them with warmth. Within these moments of silence and stillness, a moment shared here and there neither of them knew who held whose hand first. All they knew it felt and filled them with security that they have something special between them. Warmth filled their hearts with love.

Those days turned into four weeks. They began to share their pain; the pain that they had worked through, what conflicts they are working on presently, and where they wanted to go with their life. Somewhere with this sharing and caring, thoughts meshed, forming an intimacy that built into an honorable relationship. There were no demands, no expectations, and no hurry to rush into anything. They had all the time in the world.

Maxwell wanted to know everything about her. Yasmeen wanted to know everything about him. She tried wickedly to brew an anger storm within him, just so she can see if there was any and because she can. She failed miserably. He smiled at her attempt to access his anger. Really, there's nothing to be angry about, his life is terrific and he is happy. The loneliness had disappeared and he decided he wanted to be with Yasmeen, forever.

Time is theirs as the intimacy between them intensified. The days always ended with Yasmeen giving him a kiss on his cheek. Each time, Maxwell held her to him for a second longer, moving into a few minutes. Until one day, he just held her for a long time. This is how they left each other; with a smile of tender moments of trust, filled with warmth.

As winter turned into spring, she leaned over to kiss him as usual, however, this time his hands caught hold of her waist. He pulled her closer with one hand, while his other hand reached out to touch her hair then it slid round to the back of her neck, his lips brushed hers. A sudden spark of electric excitement flared between them throughout their bodies.

An urgent longing entered their hearts and they blended into one. With a low sound coming from deep within, he gently pulled her against his body; he molded her to him as his lips joined hers. She felt as sensations upon sensations rocketed throughout every vein in her body. She began to relax against him and welcome his kiss.

The initial shock she felt as he pulled her backside against his erect maleness subsided. His mouth claimed hers and first softly then urgently. Hunger sliced the compacted sun-kissed air as they seek the others' warmth. Tongues courted and mated sending messages of thirst for each other.

The ravenous hunger they aroused heightened the sensations to a deep-rooted passion that neither has ever experienced before in their lives. The intimacy was taken to a higher level and both knew they were ready to explore each other further.

Darkness shut off the last ray of sun as night fell upon them. Creatures came out of hiding and started singing in the heat of the night. All was lost as these two lovers began to explore each other. Silent messages were sent with an intensity making the warm electrifying sensations heated.

Yasmeen whimpered a sound from the back of her throat silently urgently Maxwell to deepen the kiss. He received he message. His tongue touched hers, tasting her harmony and he erupted into a growing fervor, invading her mouth more deeply. She felt the warm thrust of his sweet tongue flickering so exotically, generating an intensifying emotional rush. His tongue caressed her lower lip; she pushed on his chest as they both surfaced for air.

Lips still engaged and breathing heavy, they stayed like that until their heart rate began to subside. He gently pushed her from him and looked into her eyes. She saw his naked passion in them, shining as bright as the sun a few minutes ago.

"Your eyes are so beautiful. You capture me with your gentleness. I..... I feel full of endless possibilities. I can conquer anything," Maxwell whispered in her ear. He pulled back and drank the silent message she sent him. Her eyes sparkled in response to his, riveting them to the spot of acceptance.

Maxwell was quivering as an Arabian stallion scenting his mare for the first time. Their fierce relentlessness, over the weeks they spent courting is as if a silver blade has cleaved their desperation for completion. His heavy breathing bathed hers and felt their body united as almost one. It generated the electrifying passion that was fused with the weeks of bonding.

Yasmeen leaned her head on his shoulders and pulled some air into her lungs. His lips kissed her ears. His hand held her shoulders and softly pushed her from him. His warm sexy grey eyes sought her black ones.

"Let's go."

"Where?"

"Private, let's get some food first," Maxwell said as he held her hand walking towards her car.

"We just walked seven miles and I need a shower and change of clothes." She watched him walk away from her.

"Maxwell, where are you going? Your car is not here?" She frowned in wonderment.

He was walking to his car and then remembered he told her that he had lent it to his roommate whose car was at the mechanic's shop. What an idiot. No wonder he could not find it. He was given a lift by another officer who he was supposed to call at the end of his walk with her. He turned and walked the distance to her and said without a hint of confusion.

"Tell you what, I will go and get the food while you shower, then we go to my place so I can shower and we eat."

"What then?" Yasmeen questioned him and held her breath. She was leaning on her car as he took the keys from her hand and stood in front of her.

"We'll see."

"Oh no, we are going to make love," she inhaled smilingly. "You surprise me. Do you know how to do that?" She asked teasingly.

"No, I am willing to learn, you can teach me, you know, a little of Kama Sutra here, a little touch there." His right finger slowly touched the hollow of her neck and she trembled. "Some Tantric there," as his lips followed his finger. Her neck went back as sounds of music surfaced from deep within her lips.

Maxwell rested his back on the car, pulled Yasmeen into him, and held her in his arms. Her hands found the curve of his neck as her lips met his for a light soft kiss. He deepened the kiss, a kiss that spoke of trust and integrity, nonetheless of unfounded love, the love waiting to be discovered.

"Then I will kiss you like you have never been kissed before and you will kiss me like I have never been kissed, all over." He showed her. The laughter came from deep within her highlighting her eyes to a soft passionate feeling that sent shivers up his spine into his heart.

"And, and then mmmm I will taste you and bring you to your first orgasm and then I will possess you and we both will come together as one and we will be one," Maxwell concluded as he watched her eyes light up with pure pleasure. He felt her tremble and followed with his own. The intensity of passionate feelings was astonishing.

"I like it," pushing him away, she opened her car door.

Maxwell maneuvered her into the passenger side and as he tucked her in, he whispered in her ear.

"Let's hurry." He laughed and blew a soft breath into her ear.

On the drive to her apartment, he held her hands to her lips, kissing each finger over and over again. She tried to absorb what was happening between them and gave up because the energy of excitement was overwhelming. Instead, she focused on the short drive to her apartment building, giving him direction.

He parked her car, climbed out, opened her door, took her hand, and as she climbed out of her car, he pulled her to him and gave her a light brush on her lips. He pushed his head and looked at her. His hand moved and held her hips, giving her a passionate kiss before he turned and walked to the driver's side and climbed into the car. With no time he was driving away to the restaurant for food. She was walking into the shower.

Yasmeen can always scent Maxwell's masculinity as a mare would a stallion. Her senses became alive with passion and intensified emotions. She loved to listen to the musical lilt of his voice and how his hands roamed her body, so gently and softly. She conceded this to herself for now and knows there would be an appropriate time to tell him.

Today, she became fully aware of all of him. She wanted to feel his lips on her neck, the touch of his fingertips softly caressing her spinal cord, while looking into the warmth of his grey eyes. Then again she wants to softly caress his warm slightly tan skin, kiss his nipples while her fingers play with the little bit of hair on his chest. She stopped her imagination from spiraling out of control.

Wishes of passion throbbed joyfully within her, excitement surged forth awaiting to be expressed. She was in a short blue dress, waiting for him as he walked through the door of her apartment. He pulled her to his sweaty body and kissed her until he felt the passion oozing from them. He guided her to the door and locked it.

"Time to leave before we lose total control. Yes, I want you and I to be a "we," a couple. Are you cool with that?" He looked at her with a puzzled frown as he awaits her reply.

"Yes, I am cool with us being a couple. I like it very much. Thank you for asking." Her frankness made him relax and pushed everyone and everything from his thoughts. He held her neck as he ever so softly brushed his lips over hers.

They drove in silence, both unaware of the smell of Indian food lying on the back seat of his car. Their senses were only heightened for each other. He kissed the palm of her hand. Their hearts beat loud and rapid. The electrifying sensations became more intensified as he laid her hand on his thigh. A secretive smile touched their lips as they give each other glances of mutual knowing.

The hunger for each other sailed through their hearts like a tidal wave, leaving them quivering with intensified passion. He can smell her, as he did earlier as a stallion scenting a mare with sexual desire for his mate. He parked and took the bag containing the food from the backseat of her car. He walked around to open her door. His free hand reached out and pulled her gently towards his aroused body.

Maxwell planted a deep passionate kiss on Yasmeen. They both tremble with yearning. He held on to her hand and kissed her as they walked the short distance to his roommate Randy's house. All was quiet. No one was home. He let go of her hand as they stepped into the threshold of the flat. He put the food on the table and kissed her.

"Won't be long, put some music on, I'm starved." They both knew it was not for the food. Yasmeen emptied the food from the bags and put them on the table. She took two plates and two glasses with forks, spoons, knives and set the table. She opened a container and the spicy smell from the food took over her lungs. She nibbled on a piece of curry potato as she selected music. Barry White's greatest hits filled the air, and then she swayed her hips to the beat of the music.

This was what Maxwell walked into, Yasmeen's hips moving to the beat of the music, while her lips munched on the curry potato. He stood there, towel around his waist as water glittered off from his hair and ran onto his torso.

This was what Maxwell walked into, Yasmeen's hips moving to the beat of the music, while her lips munched on the curry potato. He stood there, towel around his waist as water glittered off from his hair and ran onto his torso.

He watched her hips move and could not stand it any longer. She scented him, as a mare seeking her Arabian stallion. He pulled the towel free and walked over to her. She turned as his hand touched her shoulders and the other reached for her waist. She exhaled.

For a brief moment, she saw his nudity as he pulled her back into his body. She felt his arousal and relaxed against his chest. She turned her head and his lips brushed hers, then he dived into the curve of her neck. His tongue trailed down to her shoulders and up again, claiming her parted lips. She trembled.

He felt the instant of surrender as her body went limp against his and he felt his body tremble. Her lips shook with passion, soughing more of what he wanted to give and is offering.

He turned her around so he can undress her. He let the halter top of her dress loose from the tie that rested upon her neck; his body now swaying with her as one. He pulled her gently against him as the dress fell to the floor. The dampened hair on his chest wet her back. He let the underwear loose next and soon that joined his towel and her dress on the floor. They picked up a rhythm moving slowly to Maxwell's bedroom.

His hands mapped the outline of her body. She turned and responded, her hands began to explore the contour of his chest as her other hand-held his neck in place; she reached up and savored his lips, matching his wants and needs with hers. Her breast heaved with a thirst for his touch and he lifted her to him. His hands cupped her backside and he entered her. She contracted her muscles as she tightened her arms around his neck, holding him in place.

He leaned against the door of the bedroom, as she kissed him on his ear with her tongue. He welcomed the ripple effect of sensations that tickled down to his manhood. He felt it and he bit into her neck as if he was a vampire wanting blood.

Maxwell turned and pushed her back firmly against the door. He heard her intake of air as she tightened her hold with her legs crossed behind his back, nowhere to go. He contracted his muscles and began a slow in and out motion. Her nails dunged into his shoulders as her head automatically fell back, screaming his name.

He withdrew from her and before she could protest, he drove with an intense passion however gently into her as his manhood touched the inner core of her ladyhood. She screamed and buried her face into his shoulders, her nails dugs holes into his back. He bit again into her neck. He scored the "g" note higher as they sang the same song of ecstasy together. Finally, they were completely one.

Maxwell's spinal cord is against the same door, holding Yasmeen in his arms, planting kisses of joy into her hair. How much time passed, neither knew nor cared. He walked with her still in the same position to the bed and they collapsed into it. He pulled her onto his body as her head rested on his shoulders and a leg on his thigh, they let the warmth of love radiate through their bodies.

A long time passed as they cuddled into each other arms, caressing as their heart rate slowed to normal. The aftermath of their love was as explosive as a nuclear bomb, as a tsunami hitting the shores, as a hurricane making its way inland. Theirs was not a natural disaster or Mother Nature's milk overflowing, leaving a path of destruction, theirs was nature-milking true love.

In the middle of the night, Maxwell awoke and reached for his one true love. Her hair lay against his arms, as her breathing made little musical notes against the hair on his chest. He moved Yasmeen onto her back as the nerves in his stomach quivered protesting hunger, pausing only to caress her breasts as his tongue played havoc on her nipples. His tongue left a wet map as he'd work his way down.

Maxwell went for her stomach tasting the hollows of curves that lay there. He explored the narrow arcs of her hips, expressing his feeling for her. He felt her stir and moved down kissing her awake. He heard her whisper his name.

"Maxwell."

Yasmeen was awakened by the sensation of his tongue exploring her skin. She tried to lift her upper body to have a look, only to be thrown back against the bed from the zillion sensations that he evoked in her body. Maxwell was scooping downwards to claim her ladyhood; the tiny nub awakened every fiber of her being. She involuntary lifted the lower part of her back to welcome his probing tongue.

His lips gazed at the fold of her ladyhood, her blood rushed to every fiber in her, sending sensational sweetness throughout her body. Maxwell's tongue circled the point of her ladyhood. He raved it over and over until she buckled with the sounds of music. She arched her back and let go with a deep sound coming from her inner organs.

He slipped a finger in her pulsating warmth as he supported her back with his other hand. He reached and took a nipple into his mouth, then back to her ladyhood. He heard her let go a deep scream of joy. The core of her sexuality offloaded into his mouth.

She panted for an intake of air as sweet exotic sensations made her blood burn with the liquid of passion. He brushed his teeth against her erect peak and felt her body tremble with more passion. She was out of control and was beyond the delight of feelings ever experienced. Instinctively she reached for his back to hold on to instead her hands came into contact with his head of hair.

She tugged at it gently and his fingers did a double stroke in her warmth, while his thumb touched the hood of her lady. She was speeding. They picked up a rhythm only lasting a few minutes. Just before she was about to climax, he released her.

Yasmeen lifted her head off the pillow in a non-verbal protest, shaking her head from side to side in the form of "no". Before she could verbalize the "no," he lifted himself and entered her in one swift quick moment. She laid her head back on the pillow totally lost in their lovemaking. She yelled out a sound that soon died as an additional one came in a succession of another.

They began to build on top of the other, making a concerto he never heard in his life. Maxwell listened and rode slow and gentle, soft and sweet. This is beyond ecstasy. He took his manhood in reversed gear and entered again.

Yasmeen trembled as the music came out from her inner depths. He joined her as she contracted her pelvic muscles and he pushed into her deeper and further. This was one heck of a hot ride. He whispered her name softly in her ear.

At last, they found a rhythm and slowly picked up a tempo, a soft gentle speed, forming their own music as his engine kept her rocking, with heightened pleasure. Their bodies slipped and slide together as silk on the skin while their hearts beat with intensifying passion and their bodies were joined, as one. They carried each other on magical wings beyond ecstasy, flying into euphoria toward a release that neither has ever experienced. She whispered his name as he emptied himself in her.

"Oh, Maxwell."

"Yasmeen, oh!"

A hundred moments later, he lifted his body off from hers. They looked into each other's eyes, breathing heavily and smiling. He rolled over on his back and pulled her halfway on him. All the barriers of shyness were cast away when their

their bodies magically joined in a union between two people, a male, and a female. She settled against his chest, breathing heavily.

"When is the next round? I lost count of how many times I had an orgasm?"

"I came once and you came twice." He caressed her arm.

"Oh, you know? When the first time, second or third? She breathlessly asked. "I lost consciousness."

Maxwell gave out a roar of laughter.

"Is your twenty minutes up yet?" she asked as her hands went to his engine and boldly took hold of it. She began revving it up and down and heard Maxwell swallow his breath. Her mouth found the hot rod of his engine as she craved her name into him. Maxwell's hands found her head as he began moving his body in and out. Yasmeen pulled away and said laughingly.

"I was just checking you out, for later."

"Oh, Yasmeen, don't tease me like that."

They are operating on the same wavelength, vibrating the same intensifying energy and it feels wonderful. He pulled her up to him, kissed her passionately, and let her go. She fell on this chest and laid her head on his shoulders. Within minutes, they both were asleep, exhausted.

Yasmeen awoke several hours later and looked for Maxwell. His space on the bed was warm and empty. She turned over, looked at the clock sitting on the bedside table, and inhaled, two o'clock in the morning. Where is he? She silently asked herself. In less than two minutes, a spicy aroma hit her nostril.

She looked for her dress and couldn't find it. She took the covered sheet off the bed, folded it in half, and wrapped it around her. This new fashion gave way to brown skin above her breast. Her thighs raise high above exposing yet more shining brown skin. She was starving and hurriedly she followed the smell. She stopped in her tracks as she saw Maxwell eating dinner, naked. She started laughing, walked towards him, and kissed his full mouth.

"I love it. Is there more, I am starved." She pelted him with a hungry smile that spelled nothing of food. He gestured and turned toward the food. She took a plate off the table and put some cold food on it, pops it into the microwave. She walked to his back, put her arms around his waist, and began kissing him. She gave him a gentle squeeze on his specialty just as the microwave ended its journey. They ate in silence, giving each other smiles as their eyes mated for another journey of loving.

Two weeks later, they had driven out to the gulf coast for a four-day weekend. They sat in the restaurant at the pier overlooking the sea. Maxwell cut into his steak, dipped into his potato with his fork, and put it into his mouth. Soon another piece of steak followed with a sip of beer.

On Yasmeen's plate sat a half-eaten salmon in almond sauce, broccoli, and potatoes with sour cream and chive. Baked potatoes were about all they had in common on their plates. The alcoholic beverage was different also, his beer to her white wine.

"Maxwell, tell me about your family."

"I thought you would never ask." He replied lifting a brow.

"I have been very busy, in case you haven't noticed. I am desperately in need of sleep and my body is overworked with too much good lovin'." She looked at him with a grin.

"Now you know why we are here." He said and took a sip of his beer. "I have three grandparents, a mother Abby, father Daren, a sister Miriam, and a brother Chad. They all live in Montana. Miriam is a cake designer and she is married to a rancher. They have three kids. Chad a website designer is married to an architect, and they have one daughter. My parents are both retired and living in the house for some twenty years."

"Have you always been in Law Enforcement?"

"No, I was once in the Marines and I was discharged due to a knee injury and now here I am." He gave her a grin and said, "I'm thirty," as if he read her thoughts.

"I know. I am older."

Maxwell looked at her and he gave what she said some thought. He thinks about their age for the first time. She is older! She doesn't look at it. He thought she was younger, he was fooled. He assumed he was older. He figured a few months. He looked at her directly and asked.

"How old are you?"

"Maxwell, I am thirty-five years old."

"Oh," he said. "That's not so bad, five years older. You know I never thought about our age until now and no." As if she asked the silent question, he continued. "It doesn't bother me and I really don't care."

"Are you sure? Five years is an awful lot for the two of us."

"I am sure, and besides I am right where I want to be, I'll rather be with you than any other younger woman."

"That's not what I asked, thank you. You are very kind." She told him and took a bite of her fish.

"What about you, Meena? Do you have any family? Tell me about yours?" He had started to call her "Meena" after their first night together.

Yasmeen took a sipped of her wine, looked at him, and replied. "I am an orphan and I was adopted by a Bajan family, you know a family from Barbados. Dad was Bajan and died when I was about nineteen. I was in college here. Mum was an American and died about five years ago from natural causes. They were an older couple when I was adopted." She took a deep breath and raised her eyes to his as she continued her story.

"My original parents were from Bangalore, India. They were visiting New York along with my foster parents when a reckless drunken driver slammed into their car. My dad died instantly while my mother died a few months later in the hospital.

"My foster parents were in the car behind ours when the accident took place. They ran to the car to help and rescue me. My mother made my foster mother promise to take care of me just before she went into unconsciousness and died in a coma."

Maxwell took a deep breath. He doesn't know how to comfort her or what he should say. For the first time in a long spell, he was lost for words. He stretched across the table and held her hand.

"I am an atheist." She volunteered and polished off the rest of her wine.

"What, an atheist?" he asked.

"It is never easy to respond to a true story like the one I just told you. You are subjective to me, therefore you don't know if I needed comforting or pity. You want to do it right, you know, no matter what you say, you will get it wrong. I've learned never to expect an appropriate response so I always add a different comment of a fact at the end, breaking the tension. Really, I am spiritual."

"Maxwell, I don't want to have any children."

"Oh, good. I don't either."

A sign of relief was released from them both and a unique sense of admiration was developed for their honesty. Respect took a higher level as integrity sank deeper into their hearts.

"Any more confessions?" She asked him.

Maxwell's only response was one of silence as he squeezed her hand. He removed his hand and sat back in his chair so he can watch the waves come ashore. Yasmeen finished her meal and joined him. The silence was a golden moment of understanding and love shared.

Half an hour later he paid the bill and guided her out of the restaurant down to the beach. Taking their shoes off, they left them on the sand above the water edge. They walked down to the water's edge and wet their feet. Maxwell pulled Yasmeen close and held her to him.

They stood there, breathing each other's aroma, as seagulls flew over them. The sea opened and blew the ocean's breath upon them as the waves washed their feet with the ocean's spray. There wasn't a dark cloud in sight, as all were smiling on the two lovers, who stood by the feet of the clear water of the Gulf.

4

Maxwell walked into Yasmeen's apartment with the night's dinner. He's preoccupied with how she will react when he tells her that he is leaving town. They have talked about what is important in building their relationship into a partnership.

Leaving town was one thing, leaving the country is a whole different matter. They never discussed this before and Maxwell is concerned even fearful of her reaction especially when he cannot tell her which country. How is she going to take it? He can feel fear rush through him and now his muscles draw taut to maximum.

He knew she was the one he wanted to spend the rest of his life with, to see when he woke up in the morning and go home to, in the night. Does she feel the same? He wondered. Long gone were the images of the girl in the photographs he had taken in Barbados. His dreams are of Yasmeen in the present moment. He made plans for them to spend the rest of their life together.

Well, he made the plans and so far, he had not voiced those plans to her nor expressed his feelings or their relationship. Darn it, they had spoken about every belief, everything they can think of and feel about nevertheless their feelings about each other has been left unspoken. Why is that, anxiety?

Maxwell could still hear her voice echoing to his wanting to take their relationship to the next level of moving in. He figured it was time and he wanted to be with her. He was surprised when she thought otherwise.

"Are you aware of how much differences we have?" She asked.

"No." He replied. "I know how much we have in common."

"It's not what we have in common. It is how we work with de differences. This will build our relationship strong, Maxwell."

Her Bajan accent seems to perk a bit. He noticed it does when she is unsure of something and totally excited.

"Oh." His face expressed shock and disappointment with total confusion.

She turned her eyes toward the ceiling, shaking her head whispering, "American men. No wonder the divorce rate is so high."

"Hold on a minute, I've never been married."

"I know that. I meant the reason why a lot of relationships go sour. It's because couples don't know how to work with the differences. They count the commonalities. It is never enough and strong enough to pull through their difficulties.

Sweethear', we've more differences between the two of us than most couples do. We have more challenges. We have to learn how to negotiate and work through our differences, challenges, and conflicts so there are no misunderstandings."

"I am….a good navigator."

"Who said anything about navigating, I said negotiate."

"What's the difference?"

"Navigating means I have to do what you want, you are navigating for me. Negotiate means you and I talk about it and when we cannot agree we take turns in choosing one wish to do and then we do the other wish. We both can share or we can do it with others or alone." Yasmeen explained with a smile and then leaned into him and give him a light kiss.

He couldn't reply; he merely nodded his head. They cuddled and watched a movie. Navigating and negotiating still circulated in his thoughts. They made beautiful sweet love, passionate as usual. Laying there in her bed, holding her, and listening to her breathing was soothing to him. It was peaceful. He felt at peace. Navigating and negotiating, Lord, help him! How can he get this right?

The conversation hit him and he began thinking seriously about them. This was the first time they exchanged words of difference, and they did not argue only exchange their opinions. Did they solve anything? It did not stack up against either of them nor was it funny and strange. They did not argue.

At least best to his knowledge they have worked through some of the differences a bit, enough to manage the present. Is it enough to hold the relationship? They are still together and there is no strangeness between them, no awkward moments, and no list of regrets or anger. This is good, it would be easy to navigate, negotiate. He bent his head and plucked a kiss on her neck. He soon was asleep.

That conversation was several weeks ago. It had been six months since they met and two months since they had made love for the first time. He remembered mentioning to her that he wanted to be a couple and she agreed, however within one month of their body joining as one they had discussed officially being a couple.

Funny, how they bought it up together after they had passionately made love. It seems the most natural thing in the world. Going into his memory he retrieved the conversation. He had said to her as his lips brushed hers. "We should be..." She had begun to say. "We should be an official couple."

"Hey, that was my line you stole. I was saying that when you chimed in." He had replied.

"Ladies first," she had grinned at him.

He smiled, a wicked little grin appearing on his face as he looked back upon their relationship. He could still taste her scent on his lips. He walked into her apartment, hoping she would be home.

Maxwell called out her name and received no reply. She's working late, hopefully, not too late. He put the bag of groceries in the tiny kitchen. They have to buy a house with a bigger kitchen in it since they loved cooking together. He opened the refrigerator, pulled a beer out, popped the lid off, and took a long drink. He washed the sweet potatoes, put them in foil, and popped them into the oven at 500 degrees. It would take ten minutes.

Maxwell took the steak and fish out from the plastic wrap, washed the steak and fish, paper dried it, and rubbed it with Yasmeen's Caribbean seasoning. He put the seasoned fish into the refrigerator to marinate. Next, he wet a paper towel and wiped his steak, seasoned it with his all-American seasoning, and let it stand out on the stove. He heated some water for the soon-to-be steamed asparagus. He took a sip of beer and walked the short distance to the shower.

A few minutes later, showered and dressed in shorts and a t-shirt, he set the table with a lighted candle and a bottle of wine left open to breathe. He added some Bob Marley music to the setting to make her relax in case she was too tired. Would she be angry when he tells her that he will have to be gone for a week or so and cannot tell her where?

Maxwell hates doing this to both of them. He can feel the fear set in. Nervousness began to take over. He took another long drink of beer. He knew the other women he dated were angry and thought he was cheating when he had to leave town. Too often, he had to pick up and leave at short notice. Follow the evidence and see where it takes you, is the job description.

He didn't plan on traveling however since he was following the evidence and it led him first to Columbia then Trinidad and next to Barbados he was more or less ordered to stay with it. He was not complaining as he was able to see other countries and experience different cultures.

A tight knot drew his attention to his stomach. He rubbed it, took a deep breath, and let it out. They both made a pact not to discuss any work due to the nature of confidentiality. He knew she trusted him from the folders of cases lying on her desk marked confidential. He had never had any desire to lift the covers and see what was written on the endless folds of papers. He watched her many nights working on her cases while he watched television waiting for her to join him.

Maxwell knew she attended some of the Intelligence meetings he now attended. At this time, they both agreed to acknowledge each other and sit separately. He also had seen how the other law enforcement officers acknowledged and treated her with respect. He had that respect plus respect plus integrity for her too and much more. Retrieving the memory of the very first time he entered the meeting room and saw her enter, he was shocked and was lost as to what to do next.

Officer Jim Taylor introduced her to the new detective that he was working with on a case. The person involved was a client of hers. He knows this how? He cannot remember how he knows this. Detective John Mackie asked her what she does for a living.

"I have a night job on OBT, you know, Orange Blossom Trail." She whispered to him. He had moved and was standing behind them when he heard her reply. He heard the whole conversation and knew about Orange Blossom Trail which was in Orlando and is filled with prostitutes' drug addicts and dealers.

"Seriously?" Detective John Mackie asked. Officer Taylor was laughing.

"Seriously? Ask him." Yasmeen pointed to Officer Taylor.

"Oh, no don't get me involved in this." Officer Taylor said to them both. The conversation came to an end and the meeting began soon after. When Yasmeen was leaving she noticed him and was as shocked as he was upon seeing her. It was later after dinner they had agreed not to mention it to anyone of the Law Enforcement agencies.

It created less complication. It was against the rules, however, it wasn't any business of the agencies. This is either going to end their relationship or take it to the next level, hopefully, take it to the next level on moving in. He was making the salad when he heard the door open. He took a long deep breath and let it out slowly, bringing his nerves under some control.

"Hi, Darlin' where are you?" Yasmeen said in a cheerful voice.

"In here." He replied, turning he saw Yasmeen laid her folders and handbag on the sofa and then step into the kitchen.

She put her hands around his waist and kissed his back. He felt his precious go straight up. Her hand lightly went up and down the front of him as she kissed his neck.

"I see your hands are full so I guess you can't figure whether I am turned on or not. And since it's full, I have the advantage."

Laughingly, she kissed him again, on the back of his spinal cord, going up with lighter feathery kisses. She kissed his neck where his t-shirt stopped and his skin was exposed. She moved to the side of his neck, then again to the middle. As she was moving to kiss the other side of his neck, Maxwell suddenly turned and surprised her.

One hand was lost in her hair and the other on her backside as he pulled her closer to his body and planted a kiss on her lips. A sharp jolt of striking sensations ran up and down her spine to her toes, then traveling up again as hot feelings of yearning spread throughout her body.

Hearts pumped louder and warm pure love poured out of them. She felt herself moistened, at the same time, making a voluntary sound, from deep within her throat, escaping her lips into Maxwell's beer-tasted lips.

She felt his hand leave her backside and then slide up her thigh, as his fingers sought the inner warmth of her moistened sanctuary. She sank her teeth into his lower lips, enough to provoke his fire, enough to make him not want to stop. She pulled back and her black eyes teasingly met his grey ones.

A burst of low husky laughter escaped him, as he drew her lip between his teeth. An intensifying electric unusual sensation ran faster than lightning throughout her body into his, and then back to her again.

A ripped current of sensuous feelings, similar to a high voltage of electricity wrapping its arm around both of them. Time stood still for a few minutes as both enjoyed the intimate moment of connection. She moved back a little so they both could breathe. After another few minutes, "I'm going for a quick shower and when I get back you'll tell me why you're afraid? Shhhhh, I felt it." She quickly and lightly brushed her lips over his and made her way to the bathroom.

Damn! She is good. Maxwell did not realize that his body carried the weight of his fear. It has been sitting on his shoulder when his Captain told him this morning where he is headed. The minute he walked into the office, his cellular phone rang. Fear kept his company. Anxiety built and his blood was frozen. He was putting salad into two bowls as Yasmeen walked into the room. The steak was grilling while the fish was in the oven. In another minute, both would be ready to consume.

"You had a long day, didn't you?" He asked her and she nodded. She had blue shorts on with a backless tank top.

"You are tired, aren't you?" She nodded again and as their eyes met, she smiled. He pulled her chair out and waited for her to be seated before he sat down, opposite her.

Yasmeen took a deep breath, a sip of wine, and said. "I'm the counselor and sometimes I become the case. When this happens, which is not often it zaps my energy. I have a very angry sexual abuse case and another kid whose father sells cocaine and other narcotics."

Maxwell's eyes lit up. This is up his alley, his job.

"I say cocaine and narcotics and you light up. Do I've competition?"

"I say anger and you light up." He replied softly.

A laugh left her. She forked some sweet potatoes and bit into it. "Mmmm good."

"And we both look at each other and we light up." He continued the jargon.

"We hear sex and we light up." She added.

"No, my love, I don't."

"What?" Yasmeen frowned and looked at him with hermouth opened in shock waiting for an explanation.

"I don't have sex with you. I have only to flirt with you outright and make passionate love to you."

"Oh."

"I see the differences, Meena." Maxwell has a serious tone to his voice, nonetheless, his grey eyes were filled with warmth.

"Oh." Yasmeen was speechless and a little bit ashamed of her thoughts. She acknowledged the differences between sex and making love. He was still looking at her when she nodded, "I'll correct that terminology. I know that sex is meaningless and making love is meaningful. Thank you." She puckered her lips and smiled at him. Her hand reached over the table and slightly brushed her fingers with his lips.

"Good. Now tell me what you can in the case of drugs." Maxwell asked her as he cut his steak and forked it into his mouth.

"Well, Mamma is trading her daughter with the present boyfriend so he can pay the bills. I have no evidence to prove it. I suspected this afternoon when the boyfriend came to pick up my client. I saw his behavior towards her and hers towards him. I have to do some more investigation. As for the cocaine dealer's son...he is not talking. Scared, he is."

Maxwell stopped eating and looked at her, nudging her to continue. Yasmeen understood. "I don't know anything except that his Dad is a known cartel, lord, or something from South America."

"Please don't think that you're under any pressure or obligation to give me any information."

"I don't feel pressured or obligated, Maxwell. We know our boundaries and have respect for those boundaries. Besides, I wouldn't tell you anything that would break someone's confidentiality or put me in danger. I usually tell another Law Enforcement Officer and I only tell him what the kids want me to tell him. I'm not unfaithful to my clients."

"Good, I guess you heard it all."

"No, sweethear', I know it all. Lik' you were in Alaqua sitting in a car with another guy. Were you doing surveillance?

Maxwell almost choked on his food. He looked up with a raised eyebrow. "How did you know?"

"A kid I counseled told me that some car was parked in this place all week and some nights, with different men looking at who come and go, like cops."

"What else do you know?" he asked.

"Only what goes on here in this county."

"Only."

"Yep, only." She replied and shoveled a forkful of fish with sweet potatoes in her mouth.

Okay, you know where the drugs are?" Maxwell couldn't resist asking.

"Not to any great extent. Most of what I know is hearsay. Maxwell love, what's your fear?"

He took a deep breath. "I have to go out of town for a few days, maybe a week."

"Personal or professional?" Yasmeen asked.

"Professional, I can't tell you where."

Yasmeen stacked her salad bowl on her empty plate, pushed her chair backward, and left the table. She turned to Maxwell. "Damn it, I am going to miss you, no, I miss you already."

Maxwell turned in his chair to look at her, his mouth opened and speechless. This was better than he anticipated. Never in his life did he dream it would be this easy. He was preparing for a showdown, a fight. This is unbelievable.

She turned the tap on to warm water as she put her dishes into the sink, she continued. "Close your mouth, Maxwell, it doesn't suit you. We both knew with our jobs what we were getting into, especially with confidentially. I knew what I was getting involved with when I decided to continue seeing you. I understand your traveling. Just come back to me in one piece." Another thought popped in her flow. She took a deep breath, "Or in whatever form. Just come back to me." Tears gather in your eyes as her voice becomes a whisper.

Maxwell lifted his full length out of the chair and moved into the kitchen, adding his dishes to hers. He put his hands around her waist, burying his nose into her hair. He loved her sea breeze scent more so when it is mixed with her sexuality.

Yasmeen stopped washing the dishes and leaned against him. He pulled back. "I was afraid. I didn't know how you would take it. How you would handle it. I may not come back." I don't ever want to be this afraid again to tell you something that's this important to me."

"Den' don't." Her accent took a nose dive into her English.

He felt and acknowledged his fear. "I want us to be free to say how we feel, even the scariest things in the most scary circumstances." He almost choked on the words. He was too emotional.

Maxwell released her and moved into the living room. Cherishing these little victories would give him the strength and courage for the next challenge in their partnership. He took a deep breath and let it out. He knew his job could be deadly. He knows more than anyone else how dangerous it can be, heavens he had lost a few buddies along his ten years as an agent. He wanted to come back to her!

Yasmeen heard his difficulty in breathing, the music stopped and the television turned on. She finished the dishes and stood over the sink. They needed some space apart to gain access to control. She let her breath out, never before had she been so close to anyone. Never before had she ever let anyone in her life or had she ever been filled with love for someone. She wanted him to come back to her!

The dishes all washed, Yasmeen walked into the living room and sat next to him. Maxwell's arms came over her shoulder and pulled her closer to him into his arms. He whispered, "I'm coming back," on her lips just before he planted a long passionate kiss showing her how much he loved her.

She whispered back. "Thank you."

They lay there for a long time relaxing into each other's body, touching and caressing. Unexpectedly she turned, pulled his t-shirt over his head, and wildly started kissing him on his chest, randomly moving her lips where ever they fancied. He turned the television off. His hand responded by pulling her top loose. She refused to let him take charge as she softly gazed her teeth on his erected nipple.

A sharp kick of desire burned from him. She felt it, and in return, her hand went into his shorts. He jumped and let out a sound that made music to her ear. She laughed.

The fever of craving for some loving began to mount as she pushed his shorts down. He lifted his backside to accommodate her, as her hand found his erected engine. Her mouth found the key to his engine and jump-started it with a huge roar. Her tongue circled his length a few times, as she jumped off the sofa and stepped out of her shorts, with a little help from him.

Maxwell laid his head back and was in the clouds with sensations of astonishing zeal. He gave up control and let the energy of wonderful bliss surge through him. He was helpless. He took deep yoga breathing because he didn't want to climax, yet. He wanted her to climax with him.

Yasmeen climbed aboard his engine and turned to the left and then to the right, up and down as Maxwell's hands held her hips in place. They were physically one. His lips and his tongue mated passionately with hers. His hand rocked her back and forth on his overheated engine.

He dove into her cleavage, then placed steamy kisses where the shoulder meets the neck, leaving a map of wetness along the path from her breast. He nipped there and there as he worked his way back to her lips. The slow steady rhythm of their bodies picked up a rapid speed as his tongue sautéed her lips.

She nipped on his lower lips. She pulled away as her head flew back and another note was added to their music, a new symphony. She was in a world of pure pleasure.

Maxwell took deep breaths as he looked at her. He was in her world of pure pleasure. With over boiling passion he let go of his steamy kisses and let her have her pleasure. He gets a high just watching her. She took over and let her body rock to their beat.

As she felt herself flying way above the clouds, she buried her face into the middle of his shoulder. Maxwell's hands held her body steady. Her teeth left a bright red mark of sharing their love on his shoulder, adding to the many others. She listened to the sound vibrating off his body and the pounding of his heart. She was beyond excited. She was running wild with his rhythm as she rode into a climax of pure ecstasy.

Within minutes Yasmeen leveled off her breath to normal, he lifted her off from him and turned her back to his chest and without warning, he entered her. His hands grounded her waist as he slowly moved in and out of her. She had another note to add to the masterpiece of a symphony.

Avidly the colossal energy of heated feelings spread through their bodies as sexual sensations rocked their core. He pulled out and laid his erected engine on her lower back only for half of a minute, giving them both time to catch their breath. He entered her again with one quick moment.

"Oh, Maxwell," she softly whispered his name.

He pulled out and reentered again. She held on to the sofa with her life and pushed back at him blending with his rhythm, she was ready to climax again. A loud joy of music escaped both their lips as they rocked to a massive explosion, simultaneously. They yelled out a melody with only their signature written on it. The bodies of these two lovers drew intensified feelings, as he went deep, pushing his rev engine, bucking wildly as he emptied his laser beams, all of himself into her well of warmth. She felt his laser beams enter her. This time she came with him in a massive internal orgasm. Maxwell hit the g-note.

With low throaty sounds, he hauled her back hard against his front as he carried their whole weight down onto the sofa, sensations rocketing through them. She turned to look to him, trying to catch her breath, however, his mouth came down on hers with a fierce breathless kiss.

His mouth drove into hers so passionately that she ended up lying across him. How that happened she cannot remember. A surge of intensified energy swept through their bodies shaking them with waves of electrified feelings. His energy generated a massive amount of heat that fused with hers. He stood up and lifted her in his arms.

He walked the short distance to her bedroom and laid her on the quilted bed. He gently pulled the quilt from under her, climbed in, and snuggled next to her. He patted her backside as he gathered her into his arms, molding her body to his own. Eyes closed they fell into a dreamless sleep.

A week and six days after Maxwell left, Yasmeen entered her apartment, and then it touched her how much she missed him. The feeling was deep numbness, leaving a trail of sadness followed by emptiness. This is what it is like to have someone share your life and then leave, hoping they would return. This is what it is like to be involved with a law enforcement officer, not knowing the outcome.

Actually, this is the same for anyone out there. Anyone can die anytime, not just Law Enforcement officers. This is the gamble in life. Once you are conscious of living life, you become aware of how precious it is so it is crucial to enjoying every moment. She never dreamed she would be wondering if Maxwell would be coming back to her alive or dead. She knew how dangerous his job can be and what she was getting involved with, nonetheless what she didn't know is how it hurts not to touch him, kiss him when she wishes.

This was a rude awakening for her. She was not old enough to miss her parents. Her adopted parents were all she knew and their love was unconditional. She mourned and had moved on with a little help from friends. She missed them terribly and guessed that was why she was surviving. She never thought of death much less living life. She had never experienced such bliss with anyone.

Maxwell taught her about living life every day. He taught her that surviving life is for people who are in pain and not living their truth. They used addictions, drugs, and material things to cover their truth and hide their pain. Who is the counselor here? This was an enlightenment that she cherished for the rest of her life.

"Oh heavens, Maxwell I miss you so much." Tears rolled down Yasmeen's cheeks. She quickly undressed and soaked under a hot shower. The tears came faster and faster, rolling down her cheeks washed away by the hot water. Before she knew what was happening she was crying profusely, uncontrollably.

Minutes later in her robe, sitting sipping a cup of tea, she was lost in thought. Her emotions numbed from the crying; she knew she is in love with Maxwell. Does he feel the same about her?

"I love you, Maxwell Halifax," she softly whispered.

"I know what I have to do, meditation," she expressed to herself. A few minutes later, she couldn't focus and plucked memories of them together. Her thoughts kept going back to the time they laughed and cuddled. She gave up the thoughts too exhausted and curled up in bed. Soon she was fast asleep.

It was three o'clock in the morning when Maxwell strolled into Yasmeen's apartment. He was exhausted after working three days with little sleep. He felt the heat surfacing from his heart as he walked into the bedroom. He stood at the door taking in Yasmeen in a white robe all curled up. He felt a knot in his stomach. He walked to where she was turned and pulled the quilt from under her, disrobed her, and found her naked body. He tucked her into the sheets. She whispered his name.

"Maxwell?"

"Yes," he answered softly.

"Oh, good, I missed you," she sleepily whispered.

He leaned over and kissed her on the tip of her nose and that was when he saw her tear-stained face. Pain hit him deep down in the center of his heart. He drew in his breath.

He just died a thousand times. A few minutes later, showered, he slipped into bed and molded her body to his naked one. He kissed her wrist with a brush of his lips. He pulled her into him and held her tight against his body. He fell into a dreamless sleep.

5

Yasmeen took the stairs to the third floor of the police department building. She waved a hand in a gesture of "hello" to some officers she knew as she walked the few feet to Maxwell's office. She stopped in her tracks and knocked on the door.

Upon hearing a "come," in a breath-constricting moment, her lips parted, she held her breath and felt the air fighting to escape from her lungs. She opened his office's door and saw him bent over reading some papers in front of him with a pen in the other hand taking or making notes, she wasn't sure.

It took Maxwell a few minutes to lift his head and receive her breath-taking smile that warmed his heart, sending it to a skyrocket high. He was speechless. She walked towards him, pulled his tie, and plucked an "I want you" kiss on his lips. She rested her backside on his desk, facing him she slightly turned resting her right hand on the papers he was reading, supporting her weight. She leaned forward and whispered.

"Nice and cozy, I say. I can do wonders here, want us to try?"

"My thoughts exactly. Mmm, however, temping that offer is, Meena you make a lot of sounds and this is a Department of Justice."

"No kidding!" At the same time, her eyes caught a photograph in a frame of a girl in a blue bikini with a blue and white batik rap. Her burgundy lips parted and her black eyes widened with shock. She gulped for air and swallowed hard, coughing. She recognized her!

Maxwell's eyes followed hers and were surprised at her reacting to the photograph. He turned to explain and almost fainted when she picked up the photograph and was studying the girl. She laid the framed photograph on his papers and turned to him, standing up at the same time.

"Do I have anything to be worried about, Maxwell?" She knew she did not however she had to ask just because a plan took shape of what she intended to do about the photograph.

"No, Meena. I can explain."

"No need to, my love. As long as she's your past, that's all that matters. I hope I'll see you in the summer. I have a surprise for you that you are going to like very much. You've to wait till summer when the waters are warm." She turned and planted a passionate kiss on his opened lips and left his office.

Under his breath he said. "Fuck, fuck, damn it, how stupid?" Mixed emotions curled up to his heart and he forgot what she said about summer. Worry took over and he rested his face in his hands. He had forgotten the photograph sitting on his desk in the months since they have been together. He had not looked at it nor even had any intensified dreams since they'd been together. Yet, guilt swept over him.

At the same time, he wanted to kick himself for not removing the photograph now that he is in a relationship with her. It was just a thoughtless gesture on his part. The photograph had become part of his life for so long and had blended into the files on this desk and had become part of the furniture. He had forgotten all about it. Having her see the photograph of the girl he had taken not so long ago in Barbados made him feel as if he was cheating.

He now stared at it from where she left it. His fingers picked it up, and put it into the last drawer, hidden from sight. Out of sight out of mind, he hoped. He also hoped it is not too late for them to continue what they have together. He wondered if she is angry. She did not look it, had not even wanted an explanation.

Maxwell made a mental note to discuss with her tonight about the whole incident. He took a few deep breaths got his manhood into an immobile mode and resumed working. He could not concentrate. He needed a cup of coffee. He removed himself from the chair, put his weight to his feet, and opened the door of his office. He stopped and sniffed the air, inhaling the aftermath of her splash of the sea breeze cologne she often wears to work. He loved her taste.

Once a while back he had checked her collection of perfumes splashes and colognes. She has a splash from Victoria's Secret called "Endless Love," another name "Anais Anais," and one that had him baffled, "Opium" from Yves Saint Laurent." Never in his life did he know of anything else except narcotics called opium. He inhaled again. Oh, how he loved her scent!

His black slacks went tight, again. He can feel the heat of his engine revving for some action, working overtime. It had been a few days since they made love due to his schedule. Once more for a very brief moment, he let his thoughts drift to their lovemaking for the last time, and just as his vision returned to him of her, he heard Peterson sniff the air and ask her.

"What's that smell?" Officer Tyrone Peterson wanted to know.

"Ty, it's Opium," Yasmeen replied.

"What the fu......" He stopped and then questioned. "Opium?"

"Go Google it and get back to me."

"Get back to you? Arrest you is more like it," he told her.

"What? Arrest me for smelling like Opium? That's insane?" Yasmeen informed him. "It's a collogue for peace's sake. Go ahead and arrest me. I have to experience this." She grinned at him. She turned on her heels and sexily walked out the door leaving the office.

The telephone rang on Maxwell's desk; he heard the conversation Yasmeen had with his workmate. He quickly took a deep breath and shut the door on his rampant thoughts. Get a grip, you fool. You're losing it. This is not the time. The ringer went off again and upon the fourth one, he answered.

After talking a few minutes to the caller, Maxwell put the telephone to rest in its rack. He picked up his cell phone, checked to see if he is wearing his gun and with car keys in hand, he left the office. He was on his way to relieve the agent who was surveilling the drug lord. He felt a tightening in his stomach.

His instinct tells him something and he feels he would be leaving again. The evidence is not adding together to put this drug lord away. There is a missing piece of evidence. He was not concerned about the traveling or the evidence; he was concerned about having to tell Yasmeen again. How much of this can she take? What would it do to the relationship?

A thought popped up and he realized that he is insecure about his relationship with her. Why? There's fear there looming in his heart and he cannot fathom what it is at the moment. How can this be? He loves being with her and enjoyed every minute they are together so why the fear? He trusted her with his life and that is saying an awful lot of him.

Pulling out of the building parking lot, his cellular phone rang and he looked to see who the caller was and stopped. It was his Captain and he knew before he answered that he will be leaving again, real soon. After a few minutes, he pulled his car close into the parking place where the surveillance was and pulled alongside his partner.

Before opening the car door, he looked around and scanned the area. How anyone can spot their surveillance here is beyond his imagination. They had found a new hiding place after Yasmeen mentioned her client spotted them. How did that kid know about them, unless it was those boys playing some weeks ago in the woods? It had to be one of them who spotted the car and did the math. He figured that's it.

This car was dark green to fit in with the landscape. There is a "For Sale" sign on the wind sheen and every two weeks they change the car color for a different one, always blending the color to the landscape so no one would suspect that they are a law enforcement surveillance team.

Maxwell looked around once more before entering the car. He was briefly on the latest development and took his position while the agent left in his car. His thoughts drifted back to Yasmeen, back to when he walked into the room and saw her curled up with the dried tears on her cheeks. He never mentioned it to her because he was afraid of what she would say and he did not want to spoil what they had together.

They had both talked about their pains and dreams; moments cherished together however they never talked about what they mean to each other. He made another mental note to do just that tonight, well not tonight soon. He had to come clean with her and let her know that he loved her. He hoped it would be easier for her when he left on this trip.

Maxwell settled in for a long night of surveillance. He picked up his cell and dialed Yasmeen's number and left a message on her voicemail, letting her know that he would be home late. It felt good to have someone to share his thoughts and life with and more so a damn good feeling to have someone to care for and who cares as much.

It felt extremely great to call her. He knew she wouldn't pick up as she was in a meeting and then she is off having dinner with some male friends, who he had not met. Is he jealous? He checked into his emotion and realized that he was not, only happy for her. They both had their own life with their friends, not that he had any friends here, only workmates.

His best friend, Damien lives in Montana with his parents, brother, and sister. Oh, hell bells it is time for him to let his parents know that he is on the verge of cohabitation with a lovely lady. He pulled his cell phone out and made the call. It was not a long call as he was working. As much as they were happy for him he was thrilled to talk to him. He left off saying they will visit soon.

In the stretch of a minute, their lives became hectic. They fell into a routine with both keeping in touch with cell phones. They kissed each other with light touches and "got to go" with Maxwell falling many nights at odd hours into bed. They seek solace in each others' arms, with each night a promise to confess their love.

Lovemaking became little "quickies" here and there with a little laughter of understanding that time seems to be against them. They know it is not however time felt that it is against them. All mental talk of the photograph of the girl from Barbados along with a confession of their love was soon forgotten.

The weekends stretched into obligations of maintaining a dual household of chores and writing reports. Cooking took a back seat to take-outs and leftovers. Friends stopped calling to invite them out and the hectic pace of work and no play took its toll.

One late Sunday afternoon, a week later in the heat of a disagreement of something neither can remember, Yasmeen walked out of her apartment into her car. What just happened she wanted to know? Her thoughts were clouded with fear and confusion as she pulled into a restaurant across the street. She climbed on the stool by the bar and ordered a rum and coke with Jamaican patties.

What is going on here? Why does she feel so unloved, tired, empty, or lost? What are these emotions that plagued her? What was the fight about? She cannot phantom a guess of how the argument started and what was being said, except hurtful words were being laid out by attacking each other. Attacking of what? This is ridiculous.

As Yasmeen swallowed the last bite of her patties, she took a deep breath and stared at the empty plate. What was her reason for the fight? Then lost in circulating a thought hit her, fear! They both were so hectic with their jobs these past weeks, she felt that they were drifting into different separate lives.

She knows that Maxwell was working long hours on this case, hoping to collect enough evidence so he can put the drug lord in prison. He never told her any of this, however, she heard through a police associate. It was frustrating for all law enforcement officers involved as the drug lord seems to be a perfect citizen, making no mistake. They don't even know what he looks like because he's always in disguise.

The DEA agents were close to having the evidence. This case was more dangerous because the drugs are laced with an additive. She knew more children and teenagers who were using it. Her cases went up more with addictions than the norm. She read the police report. There is an epidemic of overdose amount the teenagers who seem to get free access to cocaine from their parents who are the real users.

The children and teenagers were experimenting and are caught up in freebasing with their friends. This was the problem. Children as young as five sniffed the cocaine all because they saw someone did it. Sometimes the substance is carelessly left, a little residue, on the surface where the parents had sniffed the cocaine on.

Next, their children followed them doing the very same. Teenagers usually steal it from their parents and share it with friends. Her thoughts returned to her fear, fear of loving Maxwell.

Fear that they would fall into a pattern of life and just survive. Fear of Maxwell leaving her after the job is complete. She had a feeling he is leaving again. She made a mental note if he ever goes to Barbados to give him a list to bring back some of her favorite foods. It is time to face the reality of their relationship.

She paid her bill and drove home. They have to spend some time together talking. Talk about what, their differences, moving in? No, she shook her head, their love. She entered her apartment and saw Maxwell sitting on the sofa drinking beer. Next to his feet laid five empty bottles. Weariness, worry, and fear etched all over his face as he looked at her with his dark grey eyes-eyes spoken of regret and love that he found difficult to express.

Sitting on the sofa drinking his beer Maxwell cannot believe the truth of the matter. He was scared and he was pushing love away, the very thing he craved and dreamed of, he is finding fault and sending it away. He is scared to receive Yasmeen's love. Oh, he loved loving her. Giving was easy, however, receiving was difficult.

As he raked his memories, as to why they were exchanging hurtful words, attacking each other, he could not understand how the argument started. What was it about or how it turned into a full-blown fight. It made no sense, he could not believe that he cannot remember how the argument started or what he said, except it ended in a disagreement, and Meena walked out. He never thought they had any differences of that magnitude.

Now as he took a closer look, he realized he was ignoring it. He did not want to accept the differences only the commonality in their relationship. Guess it had better be now before he spilled his guts and let her know that he loves her than have her walk away from his life.

Maybe he needs to visit his parents; he sure could do with some mother's love. He should tell his parents he is partly living with a girl, which would make his parents happy. Maybe he should take Meena with him. Another thought demanded attention and he was shocked as it surfaced and took hold of him.

Who would Meena tell, talk to? Who does she have to turn to? She really has no one as her friends are social and not best friends. Thinking of it, he doesn't have anyone either. What two lonely people? Is this what threw them together? Even if it was, that loneliness had turned into love. Is he crazy? Can loneliness throw them together? Can loneliness turn to love?

He had started calling her Meena some months back, more of "Meena love" and she called him by his name Maxwell, not Max-like everyone else, all of him, Maxwell. He loved how it sounded, with a little twang of a Caribbean accent. How can he tell her he is leaving again? He cannot tell her he is going to Barbados.

Someone whose son died of an overdose wants to talk about the drugs, where it came from, and who is selling it. A female whose name is Missa Browne has a photograph of a man who she believed to be the drug lord with his son Izzy and Izzy's friend, James who is her dead son. She doesn't want to post it. She wants justice. Maxwell leaves in two days.

Stress seems to be his main name in this case. The drug lord does everything within the law and no funny stuff or unusual

unusual activities. He knows they have to sit and wait until someone falls short. Maxwell is absolutely sure that he knows that they are onto him. The drug lord can play dodge ball very well.

A cat and mouse game he has with the agents. What bothered Maxwell most is that he is enjoying himself at their expense. Sooner or later, someone will do something out of order, and he will bring the drug lord to justice. He has been doing this for too long not to understand human behavior. They always fall into old habits and do something silly then he would get the evidence to make his case in court.

He thinks of the differences between Yasmeen and him, which sprang up every time they share something together. He backs off and lets her finish or she will back off and let him finish. They never talked about it, should they? What was the argument about?

Maxwell knows they like different movies, she likes some Indian movies, documentaries, drama, cop, and robbers, while he is a true science fiction bluff. They washed their clothes differently. He put them all together in hot water, while she separates them into two piles, one pile for whites and the other for colors, and washes with cold water. He takes his laundry to dry cleaners and she irons. He never saw anyone iron here in the United States iron like they do in the Caribbean. He likes to work out in a gym and she likes to walk and do yoga.

She still goes for her walk in the evening and when he can he would join her. They split the bills in half and somehow they managed for the last eight months by backing off, sharing, and taking turns. They lived in both apartments and they have been together ever since except when working.

What was this argument about? He pondered on that for a few more minutes and finally gave in to know what it was all along. Fear? Oh hell, she must have sensed his fear and developed fears of her own or coupled with her personal fears. What a mess! He turned and saw her standing at the closed door looking at him. Confusion and fear lined her smooth brow.

"Guess this is not good for us, huh?" She broke the silence between them.

"No."

"What was the argument about?"

"I don't know," he replied shuffling his shoulder up in puzzlement.

"Funny, I wish I knew too." She walked toward him and pulled him on his feet, heading into the bedroom. As they prepare themselves for bed, Yasmeen spoke from her heart.

"Do you think it is de differences? We should talk about negotiating more, I guess. I thought we worked that out by giving each other space and backing off and sharing. I guess we have to talk about this, real soon."

"I have to leave for the job," Maxwell bolted out. He couldn't wait anymore.

"I know."

Maxwell stopped pulling his jeans off as he looked at her and asked. "How do you know?" Then he fell over and landed on his backside.

Yasmeen wanted to laugh. She thought better of it and walked over to him and gave him her hand so she can help pull him to his feet. Instead, he pulled her on top of him.

"Oh, mmm I have an inside scoop and no, I'm not telling. We exchanged information, now and again. I don't mind you going off. The first time I missed you like hell. I don't want what happened this afternoon happening again."

"Oh, Meena love, I am so sorry. I know we have lots of things left unsaid between us. I don't know how to have a relationship. Sometimes, I feel so lost. I don't want to do the wrong thing." He finally began to breathe peacefully.

"Oh darling' and you think I know about how to have a relationship? I don't either. This is new for me and I too have fears that I would do the wrong thing." She too began to breathe.

Breathing together, their breath became one. Her eyes stayed on his lips. She ran her tongue over her lips and bit into the lower one. She waited for his move. Maxwell saw that and felt his body react.

Yasmeen felt it too and she was so moistened that it ran right through from her panties onto his briefs. He felt it. They were speechless and motionless. Neither of them wanted to spoil the moment, nor not knowing what is the best alternative action to take in this particular circumstance.

They looked at each other for a long time, each reading the other thoughts and coming to the conclusion that this is not the time to make love. No, they send silent messages that they should just lie and cuddle with each other, nourishing each other with their spirit.

Yasmeen finished their thoughts for them. She voiced softly in a breathless whispering tone. "We make love then we are giving in to pain and pleasure. Let's never make love after an argument. Let's hold each other and give each other comfort, huh?" She stood off from him and extended her hands.

He took her extended hand and stood on his feet. Maxwell pulled his pants off, then the quilt over, and slipped into it.

"I agree. Let's not indulge in makeup sex." He patted the bed next to him indicating for her to join him.

Yasmeen slipped into it. He moved her onto her side and molded their bodies into one. She put her hand on the one that holds her waist and caressed it.

She let out a breath and thought that if it is not the differences, which started the argument, then it is fear. Fear of not saying the things they should be saying. Is this what their relationship has come to, fear?

She swallowed the lump that stuck in her throat and took a deep breath. "I love you, Maxwell."

She waited for a reply or even an acknowledgment. When none took place, she turned over to look at him. She smiled at the peaceful expression that lay on his face. He was fast asleep. She kissed the palm of his hand and was soon fast asleep.

The American Airlines jumbo plane touched down on the airstrip at Grantley Adams Airport on a hot day in May.

Maxwell's counterpart and friend, detective Ian Blackwood met him as the door of the plane opened. He was greeted with a "How yo do man?" They shook hands and hugged each other.

Maxwell was the first to get off the air carrier, the privilege of being an agent and knowing others of the same. Moving out of the plane onto the stairs, they walked to a different area where Ian processed his gun through customs. He never used regular customs as natives and tourists. This is the privilege he received working with other Law Enforcement around the world.

Half an hour later, Maxwell and Ian were pulling into a restaurant.

They were exchanging all the latest gossip on the island as they sipped tea and nipped on the fish cakes and sugar cakes. Ian paid the bill. They headed for the police station in Bridgetown, where he'll be briefed on the latest development on drug trafficking.

Maxwell was informed by detective Ian Blackwood that he can speak to Missa Browne about her son, James, tomorrow at ten in the morning. The drug lord's name is Adrian Del Fernando and his son is Izzy Del Fernando. He assured Maxwell that the photographs are in custody awaiting to be delivered to him.

He had no reason to doubt his friend and working mate, after all, they worked together for years cleaning the seas of drug trafficking. He had learned to trust law enforcement officers around the world due to the long hours of working together.

Cracking the code of the drug trafficking trade required the cooperation of all countries and working together as a unit. They have sent hundreds of drug sellers to prisons, however rarely a drug lord.

The drug lords have cells within cells built securely around them. They have learned how to build cells of a network interweaving with one form through several others. Knowing who the drug cartels or lords are is difficult and when known very few would mention the name for fear of being dead.

Brutal violence is the main cure in maintaining the cover and order within the organization. Hundreds of innocent people died to ensure their loyalty are kept. The web of cells is difficult to find the inventor. It takes the cooperation of countries to bring down a drug lord of this magnitude.

Adrian Del Fernando roamed the world freely. Interpol can't keep track of him nor does anyone have any idea that he is a drug lord. He and his wife give and attend charity events donating large sums of money to various charities around the world. The charity events are a façade to conduct business and to keep him in society as a law-abiding citizen.

No one would believe Maxwell that Adrian Del Fernando is the kingpin in many of the illegal drug trades. No one would believe him if he mentioned that Adrian Del Fernando is a crook and drug lord.

No, he would be laughed at and be ridiculed around town. Then there's the lawsuit that would follow to justify Adrian Del Fernando. He is going to do this correctly with no loopholes for Adrian Del Fernando to escape. Oh, no sir. He is going to nail that son of a bitch, legally.

Maxwell thought about the long hours other officers worked with him on surveillance, trying to get a photograph of this man, only to fail on countless occasions. Adrian Del Fernando does not leave home and when he does they could not recognize him. He even attended charity functions in many disguises.

Law enforcement doesn't know who to look for, making the name useless. They cannot pin a name on a man with many faces as it would stand up in any court of law. The face has to match the name.

This is a big break in a case and to finally see what he looks like is worth more in gold than anything else. Now Maxwell can put a bulletin out with a face when he gets back to Longwood. He was feeling on top of the world. Things are beginning to take shape for him. He can see the desk job and Yasmeen, yes, his Meena with him for the rest of his life.

Ian turned to his friend and said. "Ah sa man, da is a man in lov'."

"Yep, you can say that."

There was silence as both men laughed with a permanent grin on their faces. Detective Ian Blackwood has two sons from two different women. He knows about loving.

"She used to live here. I met her in a British pub. We have been

together since, eight months and not counting." Maxwell informed his friend.

"Whaaaaat a Bajan gal." Ian turned to look at his friend with surprise on his face.

"Yeap man, her mother was Robert and Elsa Thomas from Cave Hill, her name's Yasmeen Khan."

"Dam it George, the Thomases, ah kno' 'em, nice folks, a se man. I remember her, growing up here. She went to private school with the chief's daughta and Peter DaCosta. She got a beach house here, da she ren' out. Peter looks at it fa her. Nice girl."

"Thank you, man. I know she is." Maxwell said as Ian pulled into the police station. "She gave me a list of things that I have to buy for her."

"How yuh meen? Da is a true Bajan. Giv' me de lis' and I will get it for her. You'll be too buze." Maxwell opened his wallet and handed him the list with some United States currencies.

"Thank You, I appreciate it."

Ian looked at the list and started to laugh. He was still laughing as they both entered the police station. Maxwell looked at him with a puzzled expression. He had read the list and nothing funny was written on it. He does not understand what was so funny. He figured he would soon find out.

Ian announced to the entire police department of twenty personnel officers on duty. "Is gir'friend is a Bajan and sh' giv' him a lis' an' it mark breadfruit, flying fish, hot sauce and Cockspur rum."

Within seconds of the announcement, they were all laughing, all looking in the direction of Maxwell and his puzzled face. He knew the joke was on him. He held up his hands in defect and shrugged his shoulders upwards in a stance of confusion.

"Way uh seyin?" Police officer Michael Jones asked looking at Maxwell now totally lost the essence of the joke.

Ian pulled him aside and asked, "ma frien', ya don't kno" what this abou'?"

Maxwell heard the laughter in the background as the personnel officers returned to the task they were doing before he and Ian entered the room. He shook his head in the form of "no."

Ian, a bit calmer from the laughter pulled a grinning face and said.

"Is de rum man, it se cock spur........ya cock ain't spurring, ya need the rum?"

Maxwell's facial expression turned pink to red to bright red. Then he saw the funny side of it and started to laugh. If he was not a confident lover, he would be angry. This is an island joke and how the hell did he miss out on it, considering he was visiting, living on the island for so many years.

Did his Meena do it deliberately? Was it the truth what she said, she wanted the rum to make a fruitcake. She had to have known the meaning behind the rum. Why this one when there is Mont Gay rum? You can find Mont Gay rum in the liquor stores in Florida.

"Don't look so put out, man. She wanted the rum because it carries a higher alcohol volume than the States. You Yankees drink a low volume than us Caribbean people," Ian informed him.

"Oh. I didn't know that. Why?"

"Beats me. Guess you lot are more prone to alcoholism than us here. You're drinking age is 21 so what's that telling you? Plus she not knows ya givin' me the list, man."

"Point taken and thanks for the education." Maxwell gave Ian a sarcastic look.

"Ya welcome, man, anytim'." Ian grinned at him and patted his shoulders. Before he could think, he and Ian walked into a room filled with files and boxes that were marked evidence. There were many with numbers and names stacked upon each other. There were a single chair and table with a fluorescent light above for officers to work on.

"The files are on people who are under surveillance. This box is the case you are working on." Ian said in a serious detective voice. "I collect as much as I can on all the people comin' and goin' that we know about. The photograph is in a lock safe and the chief has the only key. You'll get that in the morning," Ian informed him.

"You have been really working, haven't you?" Maxwell was surprised at the amount of paper he had to read through. It would take him a few days to sort through and make copies of what he required for his case.

Not all the information would be valid for the United States only the ones connected to his evidence and the drug lords. Some of the information is only for Barbados. He was impressed with his friend's work.

"I is not as laz' as ya Yankees. We wok rain and sunshin' and don't laz' about and we parti all the tim'. Feel the energy, man. Live and breathe the lov'." Ian grinned at him.

Maxwell knew that detective Ian had the lower rank of officers doing the work and he was home sleeping with either one of his girlfriends. He also knew that when it rains no one works. When there's a party or cricket game, no one works. He also knew that Ian spoke so he can understand. He knew the Bajan accent well enough to comprehend. Ian is the best detective on the island. Since Barbados is one of those countries with the lowest crime rate in the world, there is not much to do.

Besides, Maxwell had worked with him and saw how he works; he gets the job done, effectively. When he cannot get the criminals today, he will get them tomorrow. It is an island; where can anyone run to, into the sea. Ian never worries about anything. This is the beautiful life he had the opportunity to live for two whole years.

"Thanks, Ian."

"Now man, I got something to show you, another photograph, which I didn't know about until you mentioned Yasmeen and the Thomases. It's about Yasmeen's friend Peter DaCosta.

"What about him?" Asked Maxwell feeling the muscles in his stomach tightened. His facial expression carried a blank look, however, his eyes relieved the emotion of worry.

"Here's a photograph of Peter DaCosta and some friends." Ian gave him a photograph. Maxwell took the photograph and looked at it. Ian went to his side pointing a finger at Peter DaCosta, who was in dreadlocks. Maxwell let out a breath.

"Wait, it's who he's with," Ian said with a little Bajan accent.

"Da is Adrian Del Fernando, the drug lord," Ian informed him pointing to a man with a breaded face. This is the second photo of Del Fernando so you would want a copy, too."

"What?" Shock showed on Maxwell's face as he looked at Ian with lips parted. His hand trembled slightly. His hand automatically went to his chest. This cannot be? His Meena's friend is a friend of the drug lord? What else can go wrong?

Ian took the photograph from his friend and pointed to the other man standing next to the drug lord. "The other Chinese man is a Trini man named, Ethan Franklin who is also a drug lord in Trinidad."

Maxwell had to ask the question whether Peter DaCosta was a drug lord, however before he could ask the question as if Ian read his thoughts, he volunteered the information for him.

"I don't know, Halifax, whether Peter DaCosta isn't a drug lord or whether he's dealing or selling drugs. The photograph was taken at a party. I thought I should show it to you, that's all."

Maxwell didn't realize that he had held in his breath; he let it out. What is he going to do? He and his Meena still have ways to go to have a solid relationship. Adding his fears with hers is good enough. He sure as hell does not need any more complications.

Ian continued with more answers. "The information is confidential. You can't tell Yasmeen anything. We're keeping a close eye on DaCosta and will keep you informed. DaCosta is not your problem, Del Fernando is." Ian finished making sure that Maxwell comprehended his meaning.

Maxwell nodded in agreement and comprehension. He knew his friend is not only taking a big risk in giving him this information, also his job is on the line. He could be fired. "What do you know of him and Yasmeen?" Maxwell had to ask. The muscles in his stomach contracted tighter and his heartbeat quicken.

"They are best of friends from the time they were 3-4 years old. They go snorkeling together. He owns a boat and lives on it. We can't find any income on him so we're not sure how he is living unless ya ladyfrien' is paying his bills." Ian walked to the door and turned to Maxwell, concluding his conversation.

"Pick ya up at four, read and copy as much as you can for the next two hours, then it is parti' tim' man, Bajaan style." Ian walked out of the room pulling the door close behind him.

Maxwell looked at the photograph he held in his hand. His eyes were on the middle man, Del Fernando. There was a familiarity about him that he cannot fathom at, his eyes, or was it his nose. He has seen this man somewhere before without the facial hair. Could it be the same one who is under surveillance in Longwood?

His name is Dominic de Santos with a valid social security card and he pays taxes. Is this one of the many disguises he uses? There is a long scar on his face and the wiretap in his house stated nothing amiss or unusual seems to be going on. He figured he will soon find out. Nothing he can do right now. He looked at the paperwork and figured he better get to it. The sooner the work is through the sooner he can return to his Meena.

In the heat of the night, in a darkened room a lady sits with a gentleman. The body of the lady began to sweat and swept with muscular spasms, as musical notes flow from her lips. Music the gentleman never heard before, however, indescribable sensations rocked through his body as he watched her lift the evening dress off from her backside and over her head, resting it on a bench which was next to a roaring beach.

Waters splashed over her naked body and wet her short hair. Sharp sweet sensations run from his feet, up to his thighs into his arousal, spine, and neck as he joined her in the ocean.

Open lips charter music of its own, as a hand gently reached to caress his standing ovation, which applied up and down strokes to the gentleman's equipment, heightening his arousal more than ever. He stood as erect as he can possibly be, rock-solid hard.

Inside his thoughts, the faces of the lady in question kept switching from the girl in the photograph to his Meena. He heard high-pitched whistling sounds and realized he was the one whistling and making music.

Maxwell's grey eyes popped open as he acknowledged where his hand is, and suddenly a sunburst of orgasmic sensations flooded his entire inner and outer being as he loudly roared. His hand and bed carried the aftermath of his laser beams as his body quietly stopped tearing within him. His manhood retreated to its original posture and composure. He eventually relaxed, in confusion.

Maxwell realized who the couple was, he and his Meena. He wondered if Yasmeen is having fun all by herself, missing him as much as he missed her. He laughed as he became overcome in joy. Then a frown took over his face as the girl in the photograph surfaced.

"What the hell is this?" He voiced out loud in confusion. What is he going to do? Is he being unfaithful? What is the meaning of this? He had not had any sexual dreams after he and his Meena made love. So, what was this, and more so why is she coming into his dreams? He made a mental note to dispose of the framed photograph he took of a girl on the beach so long ago.

6

It was well past midnight before Yasmeen entered Maxwell's apartment. He was in Barbados for a week and just returned an hour ago. It was good to have him home there in bed. Never mind, he is fast asleep. Every night since Maxwell left she had wet dreams.

She now knows that the face in her dreams was Maxwell. She knows that he has no idea that they are having the same dreams before they met and at the same time. He does not even suspect, the girl in the photograph that sits on his desk, that she is one and the same. How bizarre!

She remembered the time he took the photograph so long ago. She was returning from snorkeling with her friend Peter, heading to her hairdresser before she packed and headed here. If he had not taken the photograph that fateful day she was walking on the beach they would not be together.

Maxwell chose her to be his lover. It is a synchronicity that was created between them, especially when he framed her photograph and had it on his desk. The energy flows daily drawing them together, sealing their fate as a couple. The dreams will cease to exist only when they declare their love for each other. She tried once, he did not hear her. The mere thought sent shivers up her spine as the warm water hit her body.

After showering and tidying herself for bed, Yasmeen stood and watched Maxwell sleeping for a long while. She missed him. She knew he would be back. They both know they have something very special. They created it. If only they can tell each other how they feel, the fears will go away, the dreams will cease to exist. They can go to the next level in building a lasting relationship, however, it will be shaky and fall apart quickly.

The relationship is already in alignment with each other's intentions and beliefs so it's time to remove the fear. Synchronicity already played a hand and now it is up to them to make it work. They are going to have to work this through before moving in together.

"Are you coming to bed, or are you going to stand there and watch me half asleep?" A deep sexy voice sang out to her and she jumped. She laughed and climbed onto his bed, into the warmth of his arms. He pulled her into his body and kissed her parted lips in a passionate kiss. He looked at her through sleepy eyes.

Yasmeen whispered again on his chest. "Hold me, please." Her lips lightly touched the hollow in his chest with feathery kisses. "Hold me," she whispered against his warm skin. His hands tightened around her, giving her the security and love she needed to feel to stay strong.

In the months, they have been together as a couple; Maxwell always knew how to nourish her essence. Many times, they worked long tiresome hours on cases, exhausted to the maximum, where their love life was put on hold as they struggled into a safe, secure, and loving partnership. She never mentioned, "I love you" again.

She has expressed her love in more ways than one and so did he nonetheless it was not enough for them. This is neither the time nor place for a talk or affirmation nor declaration of love. It is the time to nourish each other with security and assurance that no matter what they are experiencing they can work through it.

Like right now, she can feel his erection on her stomach and knows that as much as he wanted to make love, he would not approach her. He will wait until both their essences are nourished with touching and caressing. They'll know when it is time for sharing that loving feeling. Making love is only part of the equation not the whole complete thing in their partnership.

Maxwell loved it whenever she reached for him to insinuate making love, this is a true partnership. He does the same whenever he wanted to be nourished as well. He loved being held by her. He reached for her more often than she does. He needed the cuddling and nurturing it seemed.

He cannot figure out why. He made a mental note to ask his father.

The relationship is based on quality. They both seek value within each other to negotiate personal differences. This is what has pulled them through the darkest hour of their journey together. They have learned how to give each other encouragement and nourish the relationship, regardless of the cultures and religious aspects of each personal choice.

They never took the other for granted and there is no expectation placed on either one of them. They both have expressed that they wanted to stay together and considered themselves to have a long-term future. There was one thing left for them to do, to seal their partnership, the declaration of love to each other. They have not done that as yet and Maxwell has not given her any indication of verbally expressing it anytime soon. Fear! He is going to have to work it through somehow.

Well, his Meena did, once and he did not respond in kind. He chickened out and pretended to be asleep. What an idiot! He waited his whole life to be loved and here he is with the most beautiful lady in the whole world and he cannot receive her love. He does not know how he froze instead.

Whoever said it does not matter is so incorrect. It felt terrific to be held and share life with someone who loves you and who you loved. It felt special to know that your love is cooking dinner for you after a long day.

Touching and being touched are the essence of nourishing each other and the root of a partnership. Touching and being touched is being loved. Expressing that love is more meaningful. He knows that now, why cannot he express his love to his Meena.

Damn it, Yasmeen thought, I want to say "I love you" again with Maxwell is fully conscious and I want him to say that he loves me! Damn it, Maxwell, say it; say it for crying out loud!

A tear fell on Maxwell's chest. He opened an eye and looked down at Yasmeen's head resting on his chest.

What does he do? She doesn't cry often, three times since they have been together. He never knew what to do. He let it slide. He was wide-awake now, steering up the ceiling, watching the moonlight invading the darkroom through the window, casting shadows in the shape of ghostly images. Maxwell shut his eyes as he heard a scream. Panic seeped in and images of past experiences haunted him. He saw her face; his past love in high school now plagued his thoughts with dreadful horrifying images of a young sixteen-year-old girl murdered, killed. They found the killer and this was what had driven him to become a law enforcement officer. How blind was he? He never saw her death coming.

He was sixteen years also, still a virgin. The minute his family moved into the new residence in downtown Chicago, he fell hard for the girl next door. He was five years of age and she was blond with grey eyes, just like him. They shared and did everything together, often holding hands walking to and from school. He even asked her to marry him during a barbeque in front of both families at age ten.

Listening to his Meena's breathing, lying in his arms pushed him into working through his fears of the past and anything that is tampering with his present relationship with her. He knew she was aware of his tension and fear as they lay there together and he loved her more. He felt her relax and knows she would be drifting into sleep soon.

Yasmeen felt the change in his body as the tension escalated into arousal and then lay dormant. She sensed his fears and knew instantly that it had to do with some past experiences. His past is affecting his present experiences, with her. It has an unshakable hold on him and why he cannot express his love to her.

Should she be patient and wait until he chose to let her into his past that haunts him or confront him? She chose to be patient and wait. She relaxed her body against him and felt him too relax. Yes, she will give him the time to sort through his pain and wait for him to tell her about it. What they have between them is worth the wait. She kissed his chest and was soon asleep.

Why is he bringing this up, more reliving his past? To identify the fear and address it and to work through the tight restrictions that were so mistakenly imposed upon his heart. He had to have experienced the past to be here living this life now. He had lived through that life to earn the present one.

Maxwell's thoughts went into his memory and retrieved the images of Lea replying to his proposal. She had mouthed, "Yes" and kissed him on his lips as their families' laugher exploded around them. Life took a toll for the worse.

Everything around them began to shatter, little by little. Lea's parents split up soon after and she changed, completely. Her mother went to work and her father skipped town, only to call and visit occasionally. Things were fine for a while as Lea spent most of the time with his family until her mother started to date.

Lea stayed away from him and told him she is going through changes. He understood because he too was experiencing biological changes. He gave her the space she asked for, and although he saw her every day, they no longer hung out together. He consoled himself with "at least I see her." She was always alone. Her eyes had become dark with a dreadful fear.

Rumors started to fly through the high school about "her doing drugs" and he did not give any of it much thought. He saw her each day and she looked fine, always smiling at him. He didn't understand she was hiding behind her faked smile. Then that awful day came when her mother screamed.

He had finished mowing the lawn when he heard it. He yelled for his mother and ran to their house, only to stand in shock at what he saw as he entered the house. He looked at Lea's mother, Lili, her face white from shock, and her body trembling with intense fear.

Abigail, his mother was now upon them. She too stood still for a minute and then pushed him out of the way. She covered the short distance to Lea's body which stood still, and lifeless. His mother was on her knees and put two fingers on her neck to check her pulse. She did not feel anything and that was when she lowered her ear to Lea's chest. There was no response. She yelled at him to call 911. He froze; he was in a state of shock. He couldn't move, no one moved. She picked herself up and dialed the number. It was too late.

His family moved soon after, and he lost touch with the people he grew up with, then again, he didn't make an effort. He never went back and he had no desire or intention to do either. His dad found out later that Lea was on drugs for a long time and so was her mother. Lili was the one who introduced it to her; the mother's boyfriend was the supplier. How can a mother do that to her child?

Lea's overdose was accidental, a combination of prescription drugs she was taking for depression and the heroin she consumed twice a day. Cocaine was also found in her blood and something else was laced with it. The cocktail mixture killed her. The overdose was inevitable.

His arms tightened around Yasmeen, who was now asleep on his chest. He wanted her, now. He wanted to show her how much he loved her. He has been meaning to tell her; to say, "I love you" and for some unknown God-forsaken reason, the most important words in his life cannot leave his heart, cannot be expressed.

Maxwell realized that he could not express his love for her. He desperately wants to talk with his parents, something is wrong. Why in God's name cannot he say it? He knows he loves her. He feels it every day, so what is the problem? He made a mental note to have a heart-to-heart talk with his parents about his issue of verbalizing love when he takes Yasmeen to visit them in two weeks. As he was coming to a conclusion on how best to work through his fears, he fell asleep.

In the early hours of the morning, Maxwell gently moved his Meena on top of him and then quickly turned them over so she can be at the bottom. He began slowly undressing her and with each piece of clothing removed; he planted kisses on her. He kissed her neck, moved to her breast, took a nipple into his mouth, and felt it harden. She moved slightly and made sounds from deep within her. She was still asleep.

He took the other nipple between his teeth and felt her body awakened with loud sounds escaping between her lips. Her hands moved to his back, holding it in place. She arched her back towards him. He pulled his pillow under her back, moved to the other nipple, and felt her legs anchor him to her so she can take him in. He was not ready yet to rock and roll with her. She was ready so he slowly joined them together as one.

He left the nipple and kissed her between her breast and drew back to look at her. She lifted a finger to trace his cheekbone then traveled to the curve of his lips before it entered his mouth. She lifted and connected her black warm sleepy eyes to his grey ones.

A high frequency of emotions splurged through them. Warm temperature escaped as electrifying sensations oozed out to the molded bodies in unity. He could not resist, he could not stay in control. He wanted to lose control; so, he pulled out and slowly entered her again both vibrating tremulously.

Eyes stayed engaged as she wrapped and tightened her legs around him, anchoring him into a stationary position. He lay on her without moving, enjoying the sensations that flowed from one to the other and fused them as one.

The trembling settled into a silence of passion as emotions after intensifying emotions surfaced and kindled unspoken love. They were lost in each other. His lips moved, catching her exploring finger and she felt the tip of his tongue moving softly on it.

Yasmeen tightened her internal muscles and he did the same, never losing eye contact. His hand moved under her, holding her backside in place. His other hand locked onto her shoulder, making her stationary as he pushed slowly and deliberately into her, further, deeper. She cried out and only the whispering breeze of the music she made from within broke eye contact.

She arched her back to feel the impact on her. He loves hearing her sing that song, their song. She had a new note, making the melody more passionate, more electrifying, and more intensifying.

All of Maxwell broke loose from within as they moved smoothly until they both sang the same song, of love, together. He knew she has a double orgasm, an internal and external one simultaneously because he was aiming for it. He came with one of them. He was not sure which as

he was too preoccupied himself maneuvering their rhythm. A smile tugged on his lips as he kissed her and then he lifted his body off from hers unto his back. He turned her onto her side, curving their bodies into each other, becoming one. Breathing slowed, Yasmeen found his hand, kissed the center, and whispered very softly.

"Thank you." He tightened his hold on her body. They relaxed together enjoying the aftermath of their lovemaking. Maxwell took her wrist and brushed it with feathery kisses. In a matter of minutes, they fell asleep.

The photographs of Del Fernando and de Santos were not a match. There was no likeness to the drug lord under surveillance in Longwood to the photographs of Del Fernando. The photographs were sent to a lab for further analysis. They had to wait for the results before doing anything else. Surveillance continued.

In the meantime, Maxwell and Yasmeen made arrangements for their upcoming vacation. Yasmeen had cases to close and both of them had enormous paperwork to be logged and summited. They were occupied for the remainder of time until the eve of leaving for Montana. Maxwell turned to Yasmeen and looked at her. They were in a taxi heading towards his parents' home. It has been eighteen months since he visited them just before he met her.

"Nervous?" He asked her.

"A bit, a lot, yes, I am very."

He pulled her closer, wrapped his arms around her shoulder, and held her hands. He assured her that there is no need to be because his family will welcome her. His parents could not wait to meet her. This was the first time he had ever taken home a lady for them to meet. He went into his memory and heard the voices of his parents on the speakerphone.

"Oh son, that's great. I prayed for you to find someone to love, we know she'll love you as much as we do."

His dad continued in his deep voice. "Son, don't worry, we wouldn't ask any questions. We are so excited that you have met someone. You know we'll welcome her regardless of her race. Your mother and I never brought you kids up to be racist. All we ask is for you to be loving responsible adults."

"And son," his mother chimed in. "We aren't going to mention religion or church or marriage or anything to put you two in a tight spot."

The taxi pulled up in front of a two-story tan color house. The lawn was neat and tidy with red and white flowers by the two stairs leading to the patio. Maxwell paid the taxi driver and collected the luggage. He glanced at Yasmeen, she was quiet for two days, speaking only when it is necessary. Her face was expressionless with a forced somewhat smile that did not reach her eyes. She was nervous. He was not able to ease her nervousness. He figured she had to experience his family and the anxiety will be worked through.

He opened the door with his key and the whole family was standing waiting. His father Darren held his mother, Abigail's hand, and pulled her towards them. He was grabbed, hugged, and kissed, as everyone moved him into a circle of uncles, aunts, nieces, nephews, grandparents, brother Chad, and sister, Miriam.

It took several minutes for him to glance over Chad's shoulder searching for Yasmeen. She was being kissed by his grandfather who was telling her how beautiful she was and how it is good for her to visit with them. Before she could reply, his grandmother pulled her and gave her a tight hug, and said how pleased she was to meet her. Yasmeen was blushing and overwhelmed.

Maxwell pushed every one of his family aside and walked towards Yasmeen. He held her hands, pulled her towards a sofa, and sat down. He looked at all of his family and asked. "Alright, what are you all up to?"

Maude, his grandmother walked and sat in the chair nearest to him. "Grandson, it's good to be alive and still see you." She paused for breath and continued. "With a pretty girl, I never thought I would live to see this day. Your grandpa and I were beginning to think you were gay."

Maxwell's face turned beet red and Yasmeen giggled. She squeezed his hands, looked at Maxwell then his grandmother.

"I vow he is not gay," she assured them all.

"That's a fucking relief," replied his grandfather, Andy.

"Now, now, Dad, no swearing," Daren scolded his father, gently patting on the shoulder. "There're ladies in the house."

"Well, son it's not that she doesn't know the word. At my age I am entitled, I earned it." He sighed heavenly. "I will be a gentleman."

Abigail entered the room with a tray in her hands. Darren walked the few steps and relieved her from it. She turned to Yasmeen, "Max told us you have afternoon tea so we're having tea with you. It is a little late today. I think Max got used to it while he was living in Barbados."

"You lived in Barbados?" She turned to her lover and asked him.

"She means when I was working on the assignment for the DEA."

"Oh."

"Well, I've to get the kids ready for dinner." Miriam chimed in. The twins were sitting nicely in a corner looking at Yasmeen and spoke at the same time.

"We want to have tea?" Miriam nodded and began pouring the tea for everyone, while Chad passed the cookie plate around.

It was some time past one o'clock into the next morning before the adults turned into their bed. Even grandma and grandpa stayed up however, by nine o'clock all of the children were tucked into bed. Yasmeen was tired as she showered and prepared herself for bed.

It turned out far more than she imagined. Maxwell had a loving warm family and she loved them already.

As she slipped into bed she heard the two brothers' laughter outside Maxwell's old bedroom door. She drifted quickly into sleep with a smile and warmth in her heart.

Within a few minutes, Maxwell bid his brother "see ya" and walked into the room. The moonlight was shining on Yasmeen's head and he held his breath. She was asleep and looked so beautiful. He hurriedly took a shower and tidied himself before joining her. He turned her over to the other side and curved her body to his, as one. In minutes, he too was fast asleep.

Maxwell had taken Yasmeen to visit his sister and her family in his hometown of Billings. He had mentioned to his parents that he would be taking her for a drive into the mountains on their returned trip. He wants to make love to her, and could not because there were too many demands for them to visit too many family and friends. Although they were together all the time, and in the same room, they were never alone. They were too exhausted to do anything except fall asleep.

Besides, he knew the walls would talk, as they were too thin. Yasmeen is sexually too expressive. He did not want her to be embarrassed by his family. He told everyone that he wanted to take Yasmeen to see a bit of the countryside. His mother had packed a picnic basket in a cooler while his dad gassed the car. They spent the morning with Miriam and her family enjoying late breakfast.

It was about two in the afternoon when they decided to leave and returned to his parents' home. An hour into the drive, Maxwell pulled off the road leading to an empty path towards an exclusive little area surrounded by mountains. The dirt road turned off to a cliff-like structure overlooking the town.

Maxwell loved walking to the edge and looking down. Nevertheless, that is not why he pulled nto this spot, today.

He pulled into it because he can have some privacy with his girl for what he had cycled in his thoughts since they left Florida four days ago. In the passenger seat, Yasmeen yawned and turned to look at Maxwell.

What she saw on his face made her start to laugh. This was not a picnic or view he wanted to show her. She knows that look of sexual passion in his grey eyes. She had seen it many times even at meetings where she sat across from him with other law enforcement officers. She would look up, make eye contact with him, and feel the deep passion with intensity in him. Then it would run through her.

During those meetings, she moistened and was speechless receiving his sexual energy. Sometimes, not all the time, only when time permits, they would make passionate love after they returned home.

On those days when time permitted them, they would make long passionate love, over and over again until they both were exhausted into the next day. Then they would repeat it as soon as they returned home. No, lovemaking would follow for a few days after those moments of passion.

Yasmeen can feel her body moistened as her desire took charge. She opened her arms to him, drawing his head for a long teasing kiss. He pushed the car seat back and pulled her on top of him. He held her hands as she climbed over from her seat to sit on him. He waited until she settled her weight comfortably on him and let her legs fold back over the seat.

He opened her blouse and kissed the hollow of her neck. She arched her back against the steering wheel and began to respond with earnest. Maxwell removed her tank top and threw it into the back seat, soon her bra followed and next to his shirt.

He felt her unbuckle his belt and the zipper was next. She lifted herself off from him and he pulled his shorts and underwear down to his ankles. He lifted it from his feet and they too joined her things. Her skirt was next as he pulled it up over her head and that too was tossed with the others. He lifted her onto him.

She yelled with laughter as he entered her suddenly. She welcomed the evasion of his motor revving in her special effects. She began making melodies from deep within her. It is beyond her wildest imagination. He could hear her echo coming back to them from the mountains.

Maxwell became harder if that was possible. The sensations of passion were unbelievable. Her wanting him as much as he wanted her as their bodies merged into one was beyond ecstasy. He dipped into her nipple and squeezed the other one and she responded by contracting her internal muscles. She began to rock back and forth, he lost control, and she snapped right into him. She screamed as she climaxed deep within her inner core.

He started to breathe deeply as his teeth grazed her nipples. He cannot hold out long as his ardor is far too advanced to allow her to have any preliminaries. He can only hold back so much and for so long. He waited until her breathing was a little normal, and then his lips moved over her throat to the cleft between her breast onto a nipple and then the next one. She contracted and the melody of passion meshing together in the expression of love escaped her lips.

Maxwell felt her mount swell on him and he knew she was ready for seconds. Her nails dug deep into his hard muscle on his shoulder as her body rocked back and forth over his arousal. He can feel the desires mounting to a high frequency as their bodies instinctively speak to each other.

Automatic response feeds off from them as the intensity of his hand rises hotter and heavier on her mount. She closed her eyes, felt the surge of warmth rising from them both. She welcomed his probing sapphire in her as he contracted his muscles. His teeth nip at her nipples from one to the next as she arches her back, her nails sink further into his skin.

Maxwell felt a jab of pleasure. He lifted her off from him to the tip of his arousal and gently yanked her firmly onto him. She screamed and her echo bounced back to him through the mountains. They both exploded into a fiery heated passion of pure pleasure. His echo pounded in the hollows of her ear. For one split minute, the silence was golden. He admired her essence and joie de vivre.

7

"Max love, you can't tell her you love her, because you are afraid of how she will react. What if she doesn't say it again? What if she laughed or terminated the relationship? You don't want to spoil what you have and you don't want to lose what you have." Abigail is addressing her son. She understood his dilemma.

"She said it once," Maxwell interjected.

"Well yes, she did. You pretended you didn't hear. It's in the past. Let it go for now and one day you will explain to her why you did what you did." Abigail kissed her son on his forehead. Maxwell sighed.

"Son, it is normal for you to feel this way, I did the same damn thing with your mother. I even asked her to marry me before I said, "I love you." When you find understanding in your fears, it will be easy for you to bring that moment up in time." Daren assured his petrified son.

"What?" Maxwell's shocked face was expressed to his father's admission.

"It's not a man thing, just your father's thing and you got his genes. What else can I say? No, son. It's not logical," his mother contributed.

His dad walked towards him and patted his shoulder, saying. "We are conditioned not to express our emotions because it makes us look weak. It's a woman thing, I guess. It doesn't work." Darren walked and refilled his coffee cup.

"Plus, you have a lot of fear when you had that experience with Lea. You're scared to love again coz you think you're going to lose. You didn't lose that day with Lea. You had lots of good years with her. That's how you should think of the whole experience," Abigail added.

"Why do I need Meena to hold me more than she needed me to hold her?" he asked them. He had to know.

"It gives you security. You feel loved and and nourished. You need more because of the Lea experience and emotional suppression of your job," Daren explained to Maxwell.

Meena and his sister, Miriam went to the supermarket for groceries. They are having dinner at Miriam's house and Yasmeen is assisting her. Maxwell was spending time with his parents. He told them his hesitation of not being able to tell his Meena "I love you" and along with his needs to be held. They were all in the kitchen having coffee. His mother was preparing the pot roast for the next day's dinner. Maxwell leaned against the sink as he watched her apply seasoning to the roast. She said to him without taking her eyes off the roast.

"Max, have you forgiven yourself for Lea's death? Maybe that has something to do with it. You couldn't save her and you should know by now you can't save anyone," Abigail informed him. She looked at her son for some sign that he is still involved with the conversation. She is well aware of how the male species can slip out of focus when emotions are involved.

His dad looked at him for the same reason. They both waited for him to reply and Maxwell took a long deep breath and returned their look before he answered his mother's question. His emotions are raw and high however he felt safe to venture deeper into them.

The sooner he worked through his conflict the sooner he and his Meena can move forward in their relationship. His involvement in the relationship borders on conflict of interest from his past coupled with his job.

"I thought about that situation and I think so. It was so long ago. I have forgiven myself. Every time I wrap up a case and the drug dealer is off the street, I know I am more in control than before."

"Good son," his dad replied, "I know that whole experience is behind you for years now. We just had to ask. I didn't want anything in your past to screw up the present. You are afraid to say "I love you because you think you will lose and give up control or Yasmeen will reject you. I think you feel you lost control of Lea and it was painful cos you loved her. You had no control over the whole situation. You have some now or so you think. You think that if you hold off saying "I love you" to Yasmeen then the whole situation will be different from what you experienced with Lea."

"Max, you were very young and although you loved Lea and she loved you, you have to take that chance with Yasmeen. Besides, this is a different type of love. You are older, back then you were younger. Not to say if Lea had lived it wouldn't have been true love like you have with Yasmeen. You will never know. You are entitled to love again so give yourself a break," his mother informed him. She can feel his pain.

"Abby how long was it until I said, "I love you?" His dad asked his mother.

"Oh, about two days after Miriam was born. Then again after Max was born and every night after that."

"You kept a list?"

"Only on that, my love." Maxwell watched his mother put the roast in a plastic container and added it to the other things in the refrigerator. She walked to where his father was sitting on the breakfast table and planted a kiss on his lips. He watched as his father chuckled and lit up. His mother gave him a peck on the top of his head and left the room.

His parents are loving people. He knew that they are still in love from the first time they met. Maxwell walked out the back door into a garden and sat on a bench by the herbs his mother had planted. He inhaled rosemary, thyme, and onions. He looked around and saw a little more flowers than the last time he was here. He breathed in their scent and instead smelled the sea breeze. His thoughts drifted to his dilemma of saying "I love you."

Maxwell was not going to mention to his parents that he heard Yasmeen's voice "I love you," however his mother asked and he admitted it. He remembered that moment in time and kept his emotions under control, pretending to be asleep. He lay still, long after his Meena fell asleep. The stillness and control he learned from long hours of sitting in a car, surveying people, on the job training.

He let out a long-held breath and decided that he'll not ponder on it any longer. They have two days left before they return home. Maxwell made one decision that he would ask his Meena to move in with him, more of him moving in with her. She owned her apartment while he was sub renting.

He picked his long length off the bench and entered the kitchen once more. He put his cup into the sink and headed for the stair, taking two at a time. He reached the top and walked the short distance to his old room. It was the same décor as he left it so long ago. A nap sounds great nevertheless the cell phone rang, so much for a nap.

Chad invited him to go hang out with some old pals including Damien. He went in search of his parents. He could not find them so he left a note at the usual place on the breakfast table. After many shots of liquor with some high school and college mates, Chad, Damien, and Maxwell left the bar and had dinner at Miriam's. The rest of the time in Montana was spent showing Yasmeen around town and visiting or having dinner with relatives and friends.

Within hours of being home, they became occupied with e-mails and laundry. Work took over and life kept them busy. They turned in early as tiredness crept in and took its toll. Making love was now rare as sleep was the priority. In the wee hours one morning, in the middle of being one within cuddling, Yasmeen turned over and drove her hands into Maxwell's underwear. He gasped and pulled his underwear off his hips. It disappeared with her teddy; somewhere where they would retrieve it before going to work.

She wrapped her fingers around his revved engine as he entered her core with his fingers, feeling her softness within. Lips joined as they enjoyed each other for a moment.

Once again, the melody became a song of love as she ran

her thumb up and over the tip of his probing shaft. She touched the back of his scrotum with two fingers and revved his engine into overdrive. The sound of music escaped his lips with an intensifying warmness that was generated from her touch.

Maxwell's fingers dance on her internal hot spot responding in kind. She went for his nipple and jabbered on the tip. Maxwell responded with his thumb rubbing on her external hot spot as the other two found her inner sanctuary of beauty. She added a new note to their melody as sensation upon sensation traveled into her from his loving touch. She returned the pleasure by running her hand up to his shaft then down again, picking up a tempo that matched his rhythm.

Without any warning, she rubbed her fingers around the head of his shaft then quickly down again clasping him with a firm hand.

This was it for Maxwell, he could not take any more, and he pulled

Yasmeen on top of him and pushed her down softly and quickly, down onto this hot rod, his overdrive engine. It was her turn to let out a song of pure bliss of pleasure. They felt the hot uninhabited hunger that they were deprived of for so long now surface. She welcomed his thrust and she arched right off the bed in the hotness of their fused passion.

Maxwell's hand grabbed hold of her before she fell backward on his legs, which automatically came up to support her. He lifted her up and passionately put her in place again on top of him down his standing ovation of revved overdrive engine. Yasmeen lost all control and she belted out a new song, as she bent her head and bit into his shoulder blade.

He gave her a minute to breathe before he turned her on her back, paused for a minute, entered her, pulled out, and pushed right into her again. Bodies throbbed and then he let them both cool off for a minute before he quickly with fierceness drove deeper and deeper, until she thrashed wildly on the bed.

He pulled out and turned her around. She put her legs over his waist and he entered her again. She felt all of him in her. Her body moved gracefully as if she were a slender deer, buckling beneath him. His hands held her shoulders in place and now one hand slid down to anchor her waist in place as she clutched his arms.

Eyes met with a deep intensified connection so filled with the warmth of loving. Hot uninhabited thirst oozed from them, heating the room more. In a heatwave of this electrifying passion, both bodies exploded in one massive eruption as Maxwell pulled out and pushed all of him deep into her. The wave of passionate excitement crushed every inch of them as they lay silently listening to each other's breathing.

Maxwell pulled himself on his elbows as he watched his Meena panting beneath half of his muscled body that lay on her. They were soaked in the moisture of sweet surrender. Perspiration beaded his face as his eyes caught hers. They smiled together. He turned on his back and pulled her on top of him. Lips met in the aftermath of beautiful lovemaking.

"Welcome home."

In the weeks that followed, both worked long hours and they tiredly went to bed. They were fortunate to make love once a week given the chance when Maxwell drifted into bed in the early hours of the morning. She always knew when he was home as he would mold their bodies together as one. This is a sleeping habit for them.

Many times, Yasmeen gave him what he wanted sexually as she was too exhausted to be bothered with pleasing herself or being pleased. She knows that her lover will make it up to her one day. She looked forward to those days and he never disappointed her. She also accepted that one day when Maxwell is securing he will utter the "I love you" to her. He will have to say it sooner or later because she knew she would not settle for anything less.

She decided to wait until their first anniversary. She noticed a change in his behavior. He was more relaxed with her. She enjoyed him every day rather than having him vanish out of her life. The intimacy between them reached a higher peak and they both began to feel secure with each other, more so after Maxwell asked her to move in with him.

"Maxwell, my wonderful love, would you be kind to move in with me instead?" She asked and then saw the light in his soft grey eyes. They were having dinner in a Vietnamese restaurant off highway 1792 and 50.

"Oh. That's more logical, isn't it?" He leaned over the table and gently pulled her neck to him and planted a long passionate kiss on her lips. "Of course, I will gladly move in with you." He brushed her lips with a feathery kiss and grinned.

"Why, thank you, kind sir."

They fell into a routine as Maxwell slowly began moving his things into her place, whenever time permitted. She made space for him in the closet and wherever possible. He had been living out of the luggage he used for traveling.

Weekends were spent doing the laundry, groceries, and household tasks or writing reports. They would lie in each other arms on the sofa, watch a movie, and fell asleep. Neither remembered what the name of the movie was or who was in it. These were exhausting days. The weeks fell into months as fall turned into winter. In another two months, it would be the day they met, their first anniversary.

It was a cold long day for Yasmeen when in the middle of her counseling; Maxwell was calling her on the mobile phone. It had to be an emergency as Yasmeen answered with tightness in her stomach.

"Are you alright?" she asked.

"Yes."

"I can't talk to you now. I am right in the middle of counseling."

"I have to leave now, professional and I don't know when I'll get back."

"What?" she frowned in shock.

"I am so sorry to spring this on you in the middle of counseling. I have no choice. I have to go." She heard the urgency in his voice and understood that Maxwell would never do this to her unless it was truly unavoidable.

"Okay."

"Meena?" he whispered softly.

"Yes?"

"I love you."

His phone went dead and she stared at her cell phone she held in the palm of her hand. She took a deep breath, closed it, and returned to her client. A wide smile touched her eyes and lit up her face. Finally, he said it, he said it. Oh, hell bells he said it. She wanted to dance and in her heart, she was dancing and dancing till she was exhausted.

The sixteen-year-old female client asked her smiling face. "Boyfriend?"

"Yes, he's going out of town. Can you give me a minute, please? Why don't you write down what you told me? I won't be long."

"He could be cheating on you, men are all filthy," the client stated.

Yasmeen smiled and look directly at her. "He's one of the good ones." She pulled her weight to her feet and left the room.

"I need a minute, keep an eye on her. She's in a suicide state." The assistant Li Ann nodded and glanced into the conference room.

Yasmeen took refuge in her office. She closed the door and leaned against it. Slowly, her knees buckled and her body slipped to the floor. She leaned her head against the wooden door as her knees came up to her breast.

She wanted a moment to enjoy this as long as she possibly can, right now not when she got home tonight. Oh, sweet wonderful life, Maxwell said he loves me. He loves me, he loves me, he lov.....

How long she sat there she didn't know. A knock on the door rudely pulled her out from the trance she had enwrapped herself into and was lost. She unwillingly pushed herself out from the splendor of life and opened the door. The secretary looked at her in a frown. Yasmeen silently nodded that she was well and gave her a brilliant smile. She covered the distance to the conference room.

"Where were we? Have you finished?"

"Yes, and well no. Can we tape this? It's easier to talk than write." The client's face was in pain, even her eyes were covered with deep-rooted anger. Sexual abuse cases are not her favorite, however, the anger is enchanting. It never ceased to amaze her how anger can turn into so many forms of illness and disease-carrying volcanic emotions. Hearing Maxwell's voice gave her the strength to ask the next question.

"Who interfered with you?" Knowing the answer already she waited for her reply. It came in a tiny whisper, "my teacher."

"He or she," Yasmeen asked and the reply was, "she."

She let out a long-held breath. She picked up her cell phone and made the call. It is going to be a long tiring night. It was almost eleven o'clock before Yasmeen tumbled into bed. She was the happiest person because Maxwell loves her. She fell asleep with a smile on her lips. She hugged herself and whispered. "Maxwell Halifax loves me, Yasmeen Khan, he loves me."

Another witness came forward, this time in St. Lucia. A tourist had snapped photographs of the sea and had caught two people talking and shaking hands. It caught the technician, Clive Athall's eyes as he developed the photographs. He had a funny feeling in the pit of his stomach and remembered he had seen one of the men in another photograph somewhere, however where he couldn't remember.

He called his brother, Fred Millard who is a police officer. Fred asked him to enlarge the photograph. Officer Millard took it to the forensic lab where another photograph lies in wait, to make a comparison whether it is the same person or a different one. It turned out to be exactly what Officer Fred Millard suspected, the drug lord named Dominic de Santos and Adrian Del Fernando with the same man who happened to be Trinidadian, Ethan Franklin. He made the call to Ian then Maxwell.

The photographs also put the drug lords with another known drug cartel, who is in prison in England for drug smuggling. The tourist's photograph shows also a young boy standing listening to both men. There were two different photographs with the same man with two different identities with witnesses, the tourist and a young man.

Officer Millard would leave the young man for Maxwell to unravel. He is going to track the tourist. The address he held in his palm as he drove to the hotel. Is the tourist in the photograph and the photographer related? This is the break they needed to close the case. Five years it took. This was worth it.

This was what Maxwell was working on, one piece of evidence against the drug lord. The evidence has shown the drug lords are in touch with each other. It would seal the fate of Adrian Del Fernando hence Dominic de Santos for at least a few years in prison, hopefully, life without patrol.

This is getting better all the time. Who is the young boy, his son? Now all they have to find is his son and have him testify that Adrian Del Fernando and Dominic de Santos are the one and same.

For the first time, Maxwell felt they had all outsmarted the drug lord because he rarely takes photographs. Now he has two with him. Del Fernando has many disguises and he is always on the go, never settling in one place for long. He would choose the quietest town for a while then move again, just as quickly. Even his bodyguards impersonated him, most days.

Adrian Del Fernando is never seen with his wife or son. It was difficult to find anything on him and most of the witnesses were afraid to come forward to testify against him. Providing they were never mentioned, the witnesses have

have given the police artist a hundred if not more, descriptions of what he looked like and they were all different.

They have hundreds of documents of signed testimony, however, none can be used in a court of law. It was not valid as the witnesses refused to testify against him. They were all afraid that they would wind up dead like so many others. He couldn't blame them.

Maxwell had taken all of the evidence of witnesses and created a path that tracked Del Fernando's habits of life. He became so good at it that he was on the verge of being able to predict his next place of residency. He hoped he could arrest him before he moved to Switzerland.

A person of interest had informed him that he had been there on several occasions. He had predicted Europe. He had guessed France, Spain, and Switzerland as money had left his several accounts to those countries. He had been in St. Lucia on several occasions.

Barbados, St. Lucia, Grenada, and St. Vincent were working with the United States of America to stop drugs from reaching Florida. There is massive drug addiction among Americans, resulting in overdoses and killings of various sorts over the selling of all laced drugs and narcotics.

Maxwell realized that addiction was an American problem. The answer is not an easy one. Americans have a variety of addictions and there are not adequate programs to counter the addictions. He knows the addiction problem lies with the government and not the drug lords. The logic he concluded was that if he can contribute somehow in stopping it, even for a short while it was worth it. He is not alone on this, several other countries are doing the same as he does and it helps.

On the other hand, people just want to make money and they do not care whose blood that's being spilled or how many innocent children pay a deadly price with their lives. The children pay a deadly price. His jaw tightened in remembrance of Lea.

As word spread, more and more drug lords have popped up, smarter than the last ones, more creative in hiding the money and disguising other leaders of the drug cartel. They are in every major city and they know how to live below the radar of the law. There is very little evidence that connected them to this exploitation. The users and dealers take the fall for this hindrance.

Maxwell was happy as he scanned a photograph of the drug lord and sent it to his office. Then on second thought, he decided to send a copy to his Captain, just in case one of them is a DEA or other officers that are being paid by the drug lords for information. He took the original photographs with him and left copies with Officer Fred Millard who will be testifying at the trial. He has to track the son of the drug lord.

The question remained to be asked, Maxwell voiced it out loud to himself, "Whose son are you, Adrian Del Fernando or the Trinidadian, Ethan Franklin?" The photograph only showed the back of the child's head who was wearing a cap.

Ethan Franklin is Chinese and Adrian Del Fernando is a mixture of African and Spanish heritage with a little of something else beyond Maxwell's knowledge. The t-shirt of the child had a surfer on it. He was wearing the same t-shirt in all six photographs however as much as there were clear images of the men however the child's face was not clear. The logical conclusion was the boy would not be there unless one of those men was his father.

Maybe the technician can take the images from all the photographs and put them together so he can have a composite of the teenager. Then they can enhance it to detect the time and year to verify with the photo studio. These photographs were two weeks old so that means the child is a teenager. They will have to put Del Fernando's son under surveillance and see if Franklin has any son.

The tourists were a British couple, Euan Webb, a tall dark handsome black man, and Finland Dixon, a short white man who was on two weeks' vacation. They were up early to take photographs of the sunrise when they took those of the other people.

"I was passing when Fin was on the other side of the pier and took them. I had my camera and I was walking to the other side to have a different view. "We both are photographers and we have our studio in Gwent, South Wales." Euan chipped in.

Address and information documented, Officer Millard would give all the information to Halifax who would give it to his people in Barbados who would notify the British Embassy of the couple. They would have to be checked out by Scotland Yard and give a deposition to verify the photographs. He had compared the information the couple gave him with immigration. They were telling the truth. They were not involved.

Debriefing with the chief of police in St. Lucia is in a few hours with him and Halifax. Millard was happy with the outcome. He was a regular police officer and how he has made a big connection for his country.

A celebration with many drinks would be the order and he would be hailed as a hero. Oh, yes he had to give his cousin some credit to call him. Life can't be better. After the debriefing in a few minutes, Maxwell will be on the next flight, which is at noon, and home to his Meena. He breathed a sigh of relief that this leave of absence was very short. He called his Meena and left a message on her cell.

Instead of a few police, himself, and the chief, the room was filled with one too many officers. It hit Maxwell how big this event was for the police force. More officers were there just so they can be part of something this huge. He can feel a party coming. His job never permitted him to stay long in one place much less have a committed relationship.

He wanted Yasmeen with no emotional attachment only to impress her with what a good lover he was, nonetheless the table was turned. When he climaxed inside of her for the first time he realized that he wanted more...... of her, all of her. He never felt his emotional high and knew he loved her with all of him, his heart. She taught him many valuable things about caring, sharing, and loving.

Just then another thought plunged through and knocked him off his feet. He was so emotionally shut down from his job that he had forgotten to turn his emotion on, particularly in a relationship. Lea had nothing to do with it because that was old history. He had worked through all he had to during the counseling session that his parents took him to after the death of Lea.

Her death was the reason his parents moved to Montana so he can start a new life there. His mother worked as a doctor's receptionist while his dad resumed his job as a building inspector for the same company after he requested a transfer. The other family on both sides followed them from other states and before he knew it, they were all settled close to each other. A muscle twitched in his jaw and now clenched. The whole emotional thing was a booster rocket that made his body react despite his tight grip of control. This realization surprised him.

"I've got this?" He spoke out loud as he brought his emotions under control. This isn't the time. He needed a minute for himself.

"Oh, Fuck." The admittance hit him as a ton of rocks would. All eyes were on him as the realization hit him where he was and that he had spoken out loud. He looked out at the chief talking about the case in the debriefing room and didn't hear a thing that was being said.

"Halifax, are you alrigh' man?" Officer Millard asked. "Ya look lik' ya see a ghost."

"I just realized something. I have to go. Do you mind?" Maxwell quickly belted out.

"Naw man." The chief of police Thomas Richardson assured him with a nod.

"Thank you all for all the help you give us. On the behalf of the United States of America and the DEA agency, I am very grateful to each of you for putting your lives on the line. I hope I'll get to work with you again." Maxwell told the officers in the briefing room. Another thought plunged forwards. He forwards. He must do something about those damn thoughts, he thought. He belted out, "I will bring my girl for a visit. Thank you again."

He put a hold on all thoughts as he asked Chief Richardson if he can have someone take him to his hotel.

"I need a drink." As soon as he and Officer Barrnet sat in the car Maxwell asked, "Can you take me somewhere for one?"

They were there in five minutes. The bar was a roadside one and they were quickly served a shot of rum.

"I hea' ya man. De job is stressful and de drink hel' to knock the dam' stress off the body. I hav' on' with ya. I got lots of stres'. Al' in de lin' of duty." Officer Barrnet admitted and a huge grin stayed on his face way after the drinks were delivered to them.

"I need to go for a walk on the beach," Maxwell told him.

"Tek ya tim', man. I will be bac' in the mornin' at eight to tek you to the airpor'."

They left the bar and for the next fifteen minutes, both were involved with their one thought. Officer Barrnet is thinking of the party tonight and the rest of the week. Maxwell, well, he shut those thoughts down a while back. He had no thoughts at the present moment.

"Thank you. See you at eight." Maxwell jumped out of the car as soon as Officer Barrnet pulled up at the entrance. He headed for his room in the hotel, changed into shorts and a t-shirt. He stepped out and headed for the beach.

He permitted the thoughts to plunge forward. He can manage them now. He permitted himself to think of the years of emotional suppression he endured on his job. He searched his thoughts for any neutral place he once held possessively. The place of nothingness in him, of where thoughts and emotions so suppressed that they were buried so deeply. The place where he questioned his performance of his behavior of having any regret or consideration for the consequences of his actions. If there were such a place it was gone now, banished from his thoughts.

Maxwell admitted in his line of work his emotions had to be suppressed. He was trained never to be emotionally involved with anyone or thing on the job. The deaths of officers, addicts, and people he had endured in his job performance. He never realized how this had come forward and affected him in his relationship.

How did it happen? It wasn't the lovemaking that drew him to his Meena, it's the sharing and caring she gives him, the smile, her laughter, the little things that she did for him, all wrapped up in one sensational package, a package he wants to keep forever. She had reached deep inside him and touched his heart. Unknowingly she brought his heart to life

The irony of it was that she had ended up teaching him that there is more to sex than the simple gratification of the senses. With her, it has become an exercise of thoughts together; a spiritual thing that had fed his hunger and made him desperate for more at first, however lately it filled him completely.

Touching and cuddling with her was as sensational as the orgasms. His Meena called it Spiritual sex. He had never experienced this kind of release nor satisfaction from any lover that he found in her arms!

As soon as Maxwell returned to his Meena, he's going to ask her to be his permanent personal life partner. Neither one of them believed in marriage or cared for any religion or cultural life. They both have traveled to too many countries to be one of anything. He looked back and realized that to find someone who can support you and work through the differences in a relationship is true love.

The understanding of knowing that they are both on the same side, fighting for the same causes, and believing in the same outcome is true love, it has to be, for what else can it be?

In less than a week, they will be celebrating their first anniversary of being together. A puppy would be the best gift for both of them. Maxwell knew he would mark the anniversary with a puppy. About six weeks ago, Yasmeen was admiring his partner's dogs, Seco and Bruno. He knew then that he was going to get her one. They were having a barbeque with Dana who is American and Lin who is Vietnamese. They are expecting their first baby girl in six months.

Lin had asked her if she had a puppy and what would she name him or her. Yasmeen had replied, "ah, him and his name would be Jupiter." Maxwell had gone looking for one at the animal pound and found a little black golden retriever who was one month old. He bought it and asked Dana and Lin if they can take care of Jupiter until he returns. As he looked down at the sunset from his stance on the beach, he remembered telling her that he loved spooning with her. She had given him a funny look.

"Spooning, what's that?"

He could not believe what he was hearing. When he explained to her what he meant, her body fitted into his as if they were one. She had looked at him.

"Oh, cuddling, like when we are on our sides and you pulled me into yours?" He nodded and she blushed.

He loved it when he is the reason for her blushing and screaming out his name. Then there had been other times when she said something and he was the one who looked puzzled. She had to explain to him what she meant. They had learned how to blend different words with the same meaning and make the communication work, with neither changing to accommodate the other. This is true love. They had made it work. They had learned to give each other space.

There were times neither felt like talking much after a long week. They have learned how to be silent together in the same room for hours, still enjoying each other's company. They went along all day doing personal things and enjoying dinner or other activities with friends when time permitted.

Maxwell had a few of his friends now, never mind they are all law enforcement. Yes, this is it for him. He is ready to settle into a nice little house by the beach well maybe a lake and retire with his Meena. As he turned into a bed, Maxwell realized that these last two days he had no dreams. It's about time it stopped as he was going crazy with not being able to tell Meena.

How could he tell her that he was having dreams about some lady whose photographs he had taken some two years, more or less ago? He kept her photograph, the one she saw on his desk. It seems so silly now when he thinks about it. Oh, hell bells it is still buried in his desk under some papers. He made a mental note to destroy it.

Suddenly, another thought plunged through and reminded him that the girl in the photograph turned into his Meena. Actually, coming to think of it the last time he had any dream was in Barbados when they both appeared together. He cannot tell her he was making love to her every night!

Maxwell gulped and found it difficult to swallow. He went to get some water. Oh, no. He would not tell his Meena anything. It is not worth it nor does it matter anymore. What he should be telling her in person is that he loves her. He had figured that for some reason the photograph and the dreams were connected, a mystery. Besides, he had liked the dreams and it gave him something to look forward to after a long day on the job. Now, as he closed his eyes he pictured his Meena with Jupiter. There was a smile on his lips as he fell asleep.

Yasmeen went shopping for a gift for the upcoming first anniversary. It was hard to figure out what to buy for this wonderful occasion. She walked by a baby store and unknowingly she walked into it. She never had any desire to have any children. Probably because she worked with hundreds of troubled and abused ones.

Maxwell felt the same way for different reasons. He had told her about Lea and her overdose on the way back from visiting his parents. They both didn't believe in marriage. They both had believed that gay couples had the right to be married. It is so hypocritical.

Life together had worked out for them, more than they had expected. One of the fears they had was the differences. They managed to work through the main ones, like Dana and Lin, who made the differences become more of a natural thing. They had learned how to blend their behavior to accommodate the other and now it's natural as making love.

Time seems to fly when they are together. The workload was a heavy one with long tiring days. It didn't matter as she had someone to share life with and all the more reason why the time flew by quickly. Maxwell came home to his Mena. Her thoughts turned to the times when Maxwell showed his stress.

After dinner, he drank a beer and turned into a bed, while she watched a movie or read a book. He was fast asleep when she turned in. The funny thing is, she never disturbed him and stayed on her side of the bed.

In the morning, they were meshed, spooned together as one. He does it when she is fast asleep or when he came into bed in the early hours of the morning after surveillance. She always felt him pick her up and mold her into him.

Tonight, she will hug his pillow. He has night shift surveillance. One of the tense moments she experienced with Maxwell was on religion. Well, she thought it would be tense however it was not what she thought.

"I don't believe in God and churches."

Maxwell pulled her to him and planted a kiss on her lips.

"Me, too. I do believe that something is out here bigger than you and me. It's not religious." She had given him a passionate kiss all was forgotten. They never finished the movie. As she looked back, they still haven't finished the movie.

Here she is in a baby store looking at baby things and stuff. Her eyes caught a lovely white outfit for a newborn baby and she thought of their friends, Dana and Lin. They spend most Saturday evenings together for dinner and drinks. She knows that Dana and Maxwell discuss business. Lin and she stayed away and leave them alone.

Yasmeen took the outfits and look for another color. She chose yellow, as she was sure that everyone was going to give her pink. She picked up some washcloths, a cup, and a bowl. She was looking for a spoon when her eyes caught one. It had a photograph in it, a collector's item, or a photo album. She turned and asked if she can put another photograph in a spoon.

The salesgirl replied with a "yes." She dug into her purse for a photograph of her and Maxwell. This is perfect for him to have at work or for his traveling. She imagined him going through customs with it when he worked in another country and the customs officer's face looked at him in question, a spoon? It is corny. He does like to spoon with her. Alright, who are you trying to convince?

Yasmeen was unaware that Maxwell doesn't go through customs like she does or of his future plans to be working inland. To her, these thoughts were hilarious. She laughed all the way to bed. She too, fell asleep with a smile on her face.

Maxwell walked into the kitchen where Yasmeen was preparing dinner. Jupiter was bouncing around her feet as she dropped bits of food for him.

"You spoil him."

"Ah, look who's talking, heh, Jupiter? Your master spoiled you and

me." Yasmeen gave hearty laugh. Maxwell stood behind her, his hand gently moving the hair from her neck, placing his lips on the soft skin, tasting her scent. He inhaled a midnight blue splash and tasted it on his lips. He felt his arousal as his lips traveled down her shoulders.

She said with a light Bajan accent, "you're going to have to take control of your little peter pecker." His hands replied as he held her hips into place, pushing his arousal on her back.

One of his hands moved under her dress, pushing her panties aside. She gasped and held on to the framework of the sink. The next she knew he was in and out of her. She gasped for air as he bent and kissed the back of her neck. She was in confusion as to what had just taken place.

Yasmeen turned to face him in surprise as he zipped his pants up. Looking at him she asked, "What was that?" A frown carved a hollow in her forehead.

"Relieving stress." He leaned forward and brushed her lips with a wanted kiss.

"What the hell?" she looked at him in a puzzled pleasurable bittersweet expression, bitter that the quest was less and sweet because the moment was of pure enjoyable pleasure.

He blew her a kiss, "Got ya, that's a little of what is coming later." He opened the refrigerator and took a beer out, screw the top off, and kissed her open mouth, laughing.

He smacked her backside, took a sip of his beer, and walked out the kitchen.

Jupiter looked from one to the other. This is a new movement and he does not understand it. There is not a dull moment since he arrived here a few weeks ago. The first night was a lot of noise in the room, some sort of celebration. Oh, well, he does not care. He is well-fed, spoiled, and loved. Life's a bliss.

At the crack of dawn, Maxwell turned Yasmeen over to face him. He looked at her sleeping for a while, moved the cover away from her body. He savored every inch of hers and prided himself that he knows those inches well, very well. The curve of her hips to the swell of her breast to her well-groomed pelvis and all that lies there and deep within her core. She takes pride in herself and he loves that about her.

He loves the way she dances to him in the heat of the day, slowly seducing him with belly dancing and Indian music, and the way she takes all of him into her mouth. Oh, sweet heavens, his life began when he met her!

Time to wake her up, time to have some retribution on her for what she does to his heart. His fingers slowly touched her hotspot, sitting amount the ridge of her. He played with it for a while as he watched her twiddle and swirl in her sleep.

On the verge of her being awake, he gently moved his tongue over the ridge, brushing soft light strokes. She moved, burying her head into her pillow giving out a new symphony. He moved into a position so he can carry on with his power of action on her body. His hand went under her, holding her waist in place as his mouth returned to her hot spot, gently caressing her. Yasmeen was awakened and she felt her entire being shaken with uninhabited sensations.

"Maxwell."

"Mmmm." She buried her face into his pillow, making sounds of approval. His thumb replaced his mouth as two of his fingers entered, her finding the other inner hot zone, ready for eruption. She arched her back and he slipped his pillow under her lower back, giving her support as he continued. He watched her as she bit into her lower lip and made music. He kissed her cleavage and she bit into his shoulders as he picked up a rhythm, holding her stronger as she tried to move.

Maxwell knew from the music she is making, from the sounds that she is in a world of her utopia. It will be real soon before she has her release into paradise. He can predict her coming as sure as the rivers run into the ocean. The rhythm of his touching and stroking played crazy on her senses.

Yasmeen wiggled and moved her body to the moment of his hand, and then she lay still for a few minutes enjoying him giving her pleasure. With one swift moment, she moved and her lips caught his nipple; she began returning the pleasure.

In a few seconds, she began climaxing to a height of jubilation. Maxwell moved his hand to her hips anchoring it as he boldly entered her with a rapture that took their breath away. Today, they did something new; they orchestrate a new symphony together.

Within minutes, they were both breathing the same air as they united into one. Together, the ecstasy was beyond what they both have ever experienced, separately or together. They both knew as they connected each other's eyes. In the aftermath of their lovemaking, he realized she had a double orgasm to his one. He loved it!

No words were needed, as they lay side by side, basking in the glory of the aftermath of their orgasms. He was hers and she was his, nothing more nothing less. They are aligned with each other with the pure energy of love. The love for each other had climbed another level of intimacy.

Without their knowledge, they both secretly wanted this and now as they looked into each other's eyes, knowing and smiling they felt that particular moment in their hearts. One way or the other, it will work out, one way or the other what they share, the magic, the passion, the gentleness, the love is theirs to keep, forever!

Yasmeen was invited to the Intelligence meeting because she not only

had information on various illegal activities and names to match those who are involved; she also has a knack for connecting who is doing what with who which often resulted in much evidence and arrests.

Many of her clients both juveniles, teenagers, and adults are court-ordered to take counseling. She worked with both juvenile and adult probation officers along with various law enforcement agencies, even with the DEA.

There was a series of Intelligence meetings at one of the police stations. All agencies exchanged information, discussed the best possible intervention on how to control, and managed crimes in the county. It helps keep track of criminals, criminal activities and the various agencies work together for the citizens.

Yasmeen sat with officer Perry Hinds who she has known for a long time and had worked with on several juvenile and adult cases. They had lunch together, catching up on their lives. Officer Hinds was concluding with his five-year-old firecracker son, Perry, jr's life experience.

A few other law enforcement officers joined them and they were all laughing at how wicked their children are these days. Perry, jr. was swimming with his seven-year-old brother Mel when Perry decided to urinate in the pool because he did not want to get out. He confessed at bedtime and his brother refused to speak to him.

The meeting was called to order. A cellular phone went off. All heads turned to look at the culprit because theirs were either off or on vibrate. Yasmeen turned to see Maxwell's shoulder as he walked out of the room to answer the call. How long he was standing there was a good guess. The meeting was well into half the hour before Maxwell reentered the room. He walked past her and took a vacant chair opposite her. He did not acknowledge nor did he look directly at her, however, looked he did. He stole some glances beneath the radar as she was taking notes.

They had decided to wait until his case is closed to let

workmates know about their relationship. He knew a few officers suspected nonetheless they would not dare ask any questions. He knew that they also watched out for her. Many times, he would pass on this way home or work and see his Meena and her car pulled over chatting with them in a parking lot. He never told her because he trusted her. He felt it healthy that they look out for her.

Yasmeen was laughing with them when he entered the meeting room. He stopped in his tracks and stood looking at her and all the officers. She was not intimidated by anyone, much less them. She looked relaxed and joyful. He knew that she was in court all morning giving a testimonial on a sexual abuse case. His thoughts drifted to the day before when he was in the police station talking to the chief about the meth lab and narcotic raid they did the night before when he heard a familiar voice.

It was his Meena talking to Detective John Mackie. Apparently, what he can gather was they probably bumped into each other when Detective Mackie asked her, "How's that night job at OBT working for you?"

"Huh? Oh, Fabulous. You should check me out sometime." Maxwell wanted to laugh. Here, he thought he would be embarrassed and turn red however it was Mackie who was flushed to the tilt. He had to give her credit to manage the situation.

That's his girl. He smiled proudly. He was surprised to see her now because she mentioned she would not be there. The case probably concluded early. They are going to be together tonight as it was his end of shift. She does not know that, yet.

This was the tenth meeting that they had together and someone always had a chair saved for her. Maxwell remembered the first time he sat in the chair and was told that it was being saved for someone. He was shocked when she walked in and sat in the chair. He stood up the entire hour as all seats were taken. She looks eatable. His thoughts turned to the early hours of this morning.

"Halifax it's your turn." The sergeant in charge yelled at him.

"What?" He asked.

"Where are you?"

"Huh?" answered Maxwell.

"Do you have anything to say?" the sergeant inquired.

"No."

"Yes, we do have the information we would like to share. I guess I'll do it since I'm his partner in crime and Halifax is in space and beyond. Lack of sleep will do that to you." Officer Marrows intervened grinning knowingly. Everyone nodded and laughed. No one knew whether it was lack of sleep due to overwork or sex. Maxwell turned beet red.

Officer Dana Marrows, one of Maxell's partners gave the latest development on drug trafficking, what is being sold, and the location, presently. Maxwell lifted his head and looked around to see who was listening to his partner. He turned at gave his attention to Yasmeen. His grey eyes met her black ones and they both smiled a secret smile.

They wanted to laugh nevertheless they had to control themselves. They totally missed the update on the drug lord, his name, and his son's name, Izzy. Yasmeen broke contact with him and never looked his way again. He was happy, as he had to cool down his hard drive to a soft drive before the meeting is over.

Bills, vacations, and inviting his parents to visit them were the agenda of discussion. They split the bills in half and planned to have many vacations together, visiting exotic countries. They were going to save and retire early. They opened joint savings account for a home that they are in the midst of designing. Since Yasmeen has a private counseling practice, she is more flexible than Maxwell, so they will plan vacations according to his time off.

Maxwell wanted to take her to places he enjoyed. Both agreed that the first trip would be to Yasmeen's birthplace of Bangalore, India as neither had ever been there.

Maxwell will move to Seminole County since Yasmeen has her business rooted here. He can work anywhere in the country as drugs are everywhere. A DEA agent is always in demand. His parents will visit for long weekends. They will stay in a hotel until Yasmeen and he can build their dream house.

"Build a house? That's new to me. I am so excited." Yasmeen rest her head at the back of the sofa, yawning.

"Well, my first intention was to ask you to be my lifelong personal partner. I never got around to it. Can you consider this my asking?"

Yasmeen lifted her head and looked at Maxwell who was reviewing their finances and seriously looked at her. A minute passed and Yasmeen was still looking at him. She had difficulty wrapping her thoughts through the questions. Her mouth opened, surprise marked on her face, closing her mouth trying desperately to think.

"Well?" Maxwell asked. The answer better be yes. He was sure of himself that he never once thought she might say no.

"Kinda late now, huh? I did wait for you to ask. I wanted to ask? I wasn't sure how to do it or who should do it." She confessed.

"What? I did. Oh? You want a formal asking and not a matter of fact one."

"Huh, love I am so exhausted right now. I'm having difficulty comprehending what you are saying."

Maxell moved towards her and aligned himself parallel to her body on the sofa. He felt out of synch and as he lifted her body off the sofa to stand on her feet, he put out his hand and watched as she rested hers into his, their eyes never breaking the connection with each other. He pulled her to him and held her body close to his own. He felt her warmth and was instantly aroused, she felt it too and she moistened.

"Will you please be my lifelong partner till death do us part. Then I hope you will be fortunate to find another partner for the rest of your life."

"I love you, Maxwell and yes, I will be your lifelong partner forever. I don't want anyone else, only you."

"I love you, Yasmeen Khan." Yasmeen was shocked to hear him say those precious words to her and they went to her heart. He kissed her, a deep kiss full of pure love. She pushed him from her and asked, "What took you so long?"

Maxwell still holding her hand sat on the sofa and pulled her up on

top of him. She felt his erection and whispered teasingly, "Oh, my, my, my, my, what are we going to do."

"Ignore him, you will feed him later. You'll think he never gets any…. loving." Maxwell finished and then told her because of his job he was emotionally shut down.

Maxwell talked and Yasmeen listened. This conversation took courage and she acknowledged his integrity. At the end of it all, she leaned into him and gave him a huge hug for taking their love to the next level of endurance. In the days and nights that permit them to share time together, they would christen this newfound love. They would lie and touch and kiss, looking deeply into each other's eyes.

Moments shared verbally expressing their love were timeless, passion ran deep into their hearts and love grew stronger, bolder. What is more beautiful than this? Nothing!

Jupiter lay by their feet listening to them, wondering when he would be kicked off the bed, again. He doesn't understand any of this, one minute he is given all the leftover food, loved, cuddled, taken for walks, and the next they kick him off the bed. Sometimes, he can sleep all night long, for days on the bed and he will not be kicked off. Then on odd occasions, he is kicked off, several times during the night or in the early hours of the mornings.

Not forgetting the screams and sounds they make, he thinks one of them is in trouble until he realized both might be; his barking is lost to them so now he quits the barking and goes onto the sofa in the living room. He is so used to hearing their music that he puts his paws over his ears, humans!

What is their problem? Is this how humans show their dog love? Little does Jupiter knows in the heart of his owners' passion and making love they forget about him being on the bed. Now he stands by on high alert to see what will happen next, as if he doesn't know.

Darren and Abby visited with them for a week. It was noble for Yasmeen who lost all four of her parents. She took a look down memory lane as they sat eating dinner in a seafood restaurant. Abby was sharing an experience of her high school reunion with them.

Vijay and Rana Khan were her biological parents who met in high school. They were married as soon as they both reached the age of eighteen years. She was born when they were twenty-five years old. They died when she was five years old visiting New York City. Her adopted father was a black Bajan doctor, while her mother was a white American nurse. They met in medical school in New York City.

Within three years, they moved in and were married after graduation from medical school. They were planning a family when the accident occurred, instead, they became instant parents. They told her that she gave them all the joy in their lives and had no desire to have any more children. She filled them with completion. After retirement, they both traveled and lived a lazy life in the beach house in Holetown, Barbados.

She had to learn English as her native language was Hindi. It took her a long time to understand what happened to her parents and why she is with these new people in a new home. It took about two years after her parents' death for her adopted parents to learn her language of Hindi and teach her English before she was able to comprehend the full magnitude of what happened.

Adoption was granted and her new parents never let her change her name. It was really the only thing she had of her biological parents except for their DNA. There were only some photographs retrieved from the camera in the accident, all taken in New York.

A private detective was hired to find her relatives in India. It took a year before results were found. No one wanted to come forward to claim her, because they thought they would have to take her in and they could not afford to feed their own family, much less her.

All of her parents' home and money went to her father's eldest brother as her grandparents were living there. She never received any money nor went after it when she became of age. She never kept in touch with any of them.

By then she was settled with her adopted parents who adored her, providing her with more than she is required to survive. Since her mother was an American she was able to obtain dual citizenship. She had the odd couple as parents and with that, she had the unconditional abundance of love.

One back, one white and one Indian, how bizarre was that as Peter often reminded her. She went to school on the island and made very few friends and stayed friends with Peter, her very best friend. She bonded with Peter because he did not know his parents and he lived with his grandmother until she died when he was fourteen and he came to live with them.

Later she studied in New York for her counseling degree. She was grateful for what they did for her and loved them with all her heart. They had a good life together with little conflict of any kind. She missed her adopted parents terribly. They traveled the world over. They didn't go to Bangalore because she had no desire to rake up pain plus she doesn't know her family there. She doesn't remember her biological parents. Even the photographs she has of the trip made them feel as if they are aliens.

After her adoptive parents' death, she never formed any deep-rooted attachment with anyone except with Peter and Maxwell. She looked at him and his interaction with his parents. They have love and warmth between them. She had that once and would not mind having it with Darren and Abby.

She had fun with Miriam and discussed politics with Chad while she was visiting them a while back. Abby taught her to quilt. She and Darren had shared dish duties while Maxwell was spending some quality time with his mother. It was so normal, natural and she loves every minute of it.

There was so much love in the Halifax's family, she can feel the love and felt loved by them. His dad says at the end of Abby's story, "you know son, you and Yasmeen should come and join your mother and me on our cruise to Alaska in winter next year."

"Thanks, Dad, we can't now, because we want to go to India and see Yasmeen's birthplace and visit with her family, if possible." Maxwell reached over and held Yasmeen's hand.

"Maybe you and Abby would like to join us instead," Yasmeen added as she looked at each of them. "I really could do with as much courage as I can have."

"Don't you two want to discuss it first?" His dad asked them.

"No, Maxwell and I worked that out already. It's my trip, therefore I can invite anyone I want." She chimed in with her slight Bajan accent.

"Thanks for thinking of us. We might just take you up on that." Abby chipped in.

"Don't you and dad want to discuss it first?" Her son asked her.

"No," Abby said with a frown. "I am the boss and what I say goes."

Darren leaned over and kissed her on her lips adding. "Don't I know it?" They all were laughing.

"The next time you visit us, we'll be living in a house," Maxwell informed them.

"We will?" Yasmeen looked at him with a puzzled frowned expression on her face. "I thought we were supposed to discuss it. We need to discuss it and we haven't, yet," she informed Daren and Abby.

"The architect has finished with the blueprint. We have the contractors on hold. Building the house on the land is on the list of things to discuss and we've never got to it. I've figured we can buy some land and build a house.

"I think we should take Mom and Dad out to see the land and maybe we can just go ahead and buy it." Maxwell grinned, looking at his Meena. He remembered why it was never discussed; too many hours spent making love to her.

His parents did not miss the implication as to why buying the land was never discussed. It is all very familiar with them; half of a conversation here and the other half another time or totally forgotten. Misunderstandings came into effect on hundreds of occasions, where they too left to make love, and the discussion was long forgotten until assumptions were made in error that they thought they had the discussion.

Abby reached for her husband's hand as they looked at their son and Yasmeen talking about the land they want to purchase and the house they are going to build, soon, they were happy for their son. The worrying was over. This love is as special and as real as what she and Darren shared. Their son had finally found love and a wonderful girl to return his love. She was thrilled as she squeezed Daren's hand and smiled at him. He too can experience the love his son shared with Yasmeen.

He is as happy as his wife that his son finally found a loving girl to love. They were worried about him for a long time and even though like Maxwell's grandparents that he might be gay, and even if he were, they would have accepted it. It would not have mattered whom he choose for his life partner just as long as he was happy.

"Well," Abby interrupted them. "You both know what you want and that's good. It took us a while to know what we wanted. We had long conversations late into the night and continued into the next day, many topics left not discussed."

"It took us months to decide and we look at about twenty houses before we settled on the one we live in," Daren said.

"I like yours. It's warm and cozy," Yasmeen said.

"Yes, it is thank you." Maxwell put his arm around her shoulder, pulling her to him, and planted a kiss on her ear.

The waitress arrived and Daren paid the bill. Maxwell left a tip. He hauled his length up and pulled Yasmeen's chair as she rose on her feet. Yasmeen turned to both Daren and Abby.

"Thanks for dinner. It was great to have both of you here with us. Please put us in on regular visits. When we have our home you both can stay with us."

"Don't you want to discuss this with my son?" Abby laughing said. They all head to the stairs into the night. They had dinner at the hotel where Abby and Daren are staying. They are leaving in the morning for the airport.

"No, your son would agree with me on this one. There's no need in discussing it, right honey?" Yasmeen looked at Maxwell for confirmation.

Maxwell squeezed her hands. "She's the boss. You taught her well for the short time she spent with you, Mom."

They were still laughing as the valet pulled up with Maxwell's car. Yasmeen and Maxwell hugged and kissed them both. They hugged and kissed their son and whispered, "I love you," in his ear. Something they shared with their children.

Maxwell stepped back and took up his place next to Yasmeen as he held her hands. They waved to his parents as he saw his Meena into the passenger's seat. Daren and Abby gave them a final wave before they walked into the hotel door. They stopped and turned as they saw their son drive off with his Meena. They love her already.

9

"You can't do that," Maxwell told her. They were standing in the middle of his office.

"Oh yes I can," Yasmeen replied. "It's illegal. I can't tell you where the illegal drugs are being kept, because what my client says is confidential. He's covered under my protection until he violates the laws then I can talk. Until then my lips are sealed. You can question him with his lawyer present. I told him not to say anything until a lawyer is present or I am. I told him when he's questioned by Law Enforcement quietly demand a lawyer."

Maxwell pulled his length off the table he was leaning against and very quietly said to her in an attacking voice.

"Lady, you are way out of line. I've worked long hard dark hours, crossing the ocean collecting hardcore evidence on this drug dealer and you just can't walk in here and make it fall apart, I won't allow it." His used-to-be soft grey eyes turned into deep dark grey furious ones. His jaw twitched uncontrollably. His body tensed with anger.

"It's not for you to allow. He's a child, Maxwell and his rights come first. I want to make him see what his father is and help him through it before he testifies against him. It's his father. He has to be protected. You understand that, don't you?" Yasmeen pleaded with Maxwell.

"No deal."

Yasmeen quickly shoved all frustration aside as a new burst of fury flashed in her black eyes. The look she gave him was heartless and now confusion pushed through once again overriding the frustration and fury she is feeling in her heart. She cannot believe his heartlessness.

"Maxwell, go ahead and try. You know the only way this can be legal is when he has an adult present with him. I am his counselor and I say no." Yasmeen turned and walked a foot away, leaving Maxwell shocked and confused. She walked over to him covering the distance between them within five seconds. She stood looking into his dark gray eyes at the same time bringing with her the scent of morning mist from a waterfall on a hot summer night.

His body temperature could do with some lowering due to the anger that engulfed him. It did for a spur of a moment then once again fear crept in again reminding him as to why he was afraid. He took his stance against the situation, however never against her. If she could only slant the information in his favor, all will be well.

Then there is the son, her client who would be hurt badly. Yes, he sees her logic and a touch of love surfaced and he knew it would be her way and not his all in the name of a teenager.

"Oh, Maxwell, just for your information, I don't cheat, neither do I buckle under fear, or intimation, you of all people should know that."

Maxwell opened his mouth to speak and Yasmeen continued before he said anything, in a deep Bajan accent, indicating she was more confused than angry. "It's not about you, it is about that lost kid in de detention center, who's been mentally raped repeatedly by everyone, I let you in, you'll do the same, making no different like all the rest of those who mentally, verbally, emotionally raped him.

"He'll never be able to survive, no matter how much therapy we give him. He'll never be the same. With me, I can nourish his spirit, get him back into society, and then he can tell you whatever you want to know. How long it takes, I don't know. We'll have to wait and see." She spoke softly and firmly.

Yasmeen wanted to laugh at his anger. How dare he questioned her about her client. Oh, she loved him more with each passing day, nevertheless, this was the first time that they have been together and they've had this professional disagreement and she hates it. This conflict of interest in their personal lives is now pushing against their professional lives, what a hoot?

Maxwell is thinking about all the teenagers he would be saving and she is thinking about this one and only one teenager who is devastated to discover that his father was responsible for killing thousands of people with his drug trade. Everything he has was bought for him with blood money.

Yasmeen wondered how long it would take him to cool down. His eyes dance with rage and looked dangerous. Then it hit her, this is not about the case. Her lover has a fear of something that she can't phantom a guess. She would not believe it. Something is covering his situation and she doesn't know what is bothering him.

She had seen his eyes deepen with color many times during making love to her and also when he is passionate about something. It now has the same color, however, this is somehow different, love yes under the fear and anger. She knows the differences between passion and anger.

These two emotions share the same cocoon and carry similar traits, making them a target for mistaken identity, pleasure, and pain, creating confusion with others who do not know the differences. Love and anger emotions can easily build into pain and pleasure.

Love and anger are on the opposite side of the spectrum of emotions. Often desire is accompanied by passion then joy follows, while suppression is accompanied by anger then violence. This is what most relationships live on.

Maxwell's fear is showing under his rage. What is he afraid of? Why did he not say what it is? Now, he has to move out and live temporarily until this matter is settled. For this to be uniformly legal and acceptable in court, the evidence has to show that it was not corroded and manipulated. They cannot be involved with each other. How is he going to manage? How is she going to manage?

If anything surfaced about their relationship in the Criminal Justice System the minute the court found out that they were representing opposite sides and they were no longer involved as a couple, the evidence is not compromised. Yasmeen was in the elevator when a handheld the door from closing. She took a deep long breath as soon as she made eye contact with Maxwell.

"No, no deal," he shouted angrily in front of her and quietly, so no one can hear them. Nevertheless, all eyes were on the pair of them. You could hear a pin drop. She whispered and he had to lean closer to hear her words.

"You have no choice. He's the key to sealing your deal, I agree. I'll tell you what I know now, you'll not only kill him, you will also kill me, too. When word gets out on the street that I betrayed Izzy Del Fernando, they are going to come after me. I am dead. I love my life...." She thinks and I love you. She continued. "I want to live and I would've thought that you would want the same for me too."

"I can protect you."

"Oh, no you can't. No one can protect me. You don't get it, I am alive because I am the only one who understands these kids. I take their pain away. I keep their secrets and I get them to see that crimes are not the way to live life.

"I am their hope for the future. I'll never cheat much less betray them. I know of a way I can silently contribute to the case you are working on without any of the kids knowing that I am involved in."

"No, the case is not going to hold up in court. I want to know what he knows so I can go and get the drugs off the streets. I can't wait. It wouldn't work. The only way it can hold up in court and the drug dealers and lord can be put away is doing it my way, so give me the address as to where the drugs are being held," Maxwell desperately informed her. Why can't she see the sooner it is over the sooner they would be together?

"No, I can't do that, and no, you can't arrest me for obstructing an investigation, nor can you get a court order for me to talk because I don't have the address. I can get it and you cannot. We've to do it my way. I can hazard a good guess and I am never wrong.

"Besides, these kids grew up poor and unwanted by parents and society. They either learn how to survive in life or drop out of life. They turn to a life of crime through the gangs

gangs and drugs they sell for food. They are already dead internally. Why can't you see that?" She pleaded with him.

"It doesn't work like that, you're a fool. I can protect you. You are going to let the drug dealer and lord go and all the months of work my buddies and I did will go up in smoke, just because of your selfishness."

She inhaled deeply and let it out. "My way or no deal."

"No deal." He responded in rage. Rage ate into his words as his

eyes glinted dangerously.

"I guess you don't really care if I ended up dead, so much for love. I don't need protection I need security." She blinked the tears that brimmed in her eyes, walked past him out of the elevator, heading for the door to the stairs.

Maxwell was left staring after her. This static cannot be measured because his accusation ran deeply into old wounds that he thought he had let go of. He knew that he was pushing her away with his fears. He waited this long to get the bloody drug lord; he could have waited and played it her way. He was angry with himself. He knew he cannot protect her and that is what is killing him.

All his life he was taught to protect and serve. He protected and served everyone. He cannot protect the one person whose trade winds warm his heart, the one person he loved and his only love. It scares the hell out of him and he is lost as to what to do.

He turned and walked back into his office. He sat in his chair and put his head into his hands. He knows she is right and he feels it too. Maxwell's desires for protecting her were his seed of love that he had planted in them. It didn't flourish. She doesn't need protection she needs security. Oh, doggone it. What does that mean? First, it was negotiating versus what? He cannot remember, protection versus security.

Security for what, love, trust? He looked back as to how it all started two days ago when Yasmeen walked into the Intelligence meeting that had commenced thirty minutes early. All eyes turned to see who it was and she looked at

Lieutenant Bailey who was explaining what they had so far on the drug lord, "Sorry."

Instead of her finding a seat Yasmeen headed for the board with all the photographs with notes stapled on. She pulled a few off and rearranged them in a different order. The meeting was put on hold or rather Lieutenant Bailey put his words on freeze as his eyes followed her.

She pointed to the photographs, "This one's when Izzy was five years, these two ten years and this one sixteen years. He loves that t-shirt so much his father had it made in six of his favorite colors and all different sizes. What're all these photographs doing here with your lot?"

"You know the kid?" Lieutenant Bailey asked. Maxwell was too shocked to say anything. He couldn't believe what he was hearing.

"Yes, his mother brought him to me because his grades have dropped and he's in company with the wrong kids in school. What's the "wrong kids" is beyond my comprehension," Yasmeen informed them.

"What's his name?" asked Lieutenant Bailey.

"Izzy de Soto. He has his mother's name. I don't know anything about his father. He lives in mmm.... I don't remember. I can give you his address providing I know what it's for."

"Where were you when we mentioned his name at the last meeting?

Daydreaming?" Seeing her blush and answered his question. "Never mind, don't answer. Izzy's father is this man we think." Lieutenant Bailey pointed to Adrian Del Fernando, "he's the drug lord that Halifax was tracking for the last five years.

"Halifax!" Yasmeen was the one who was in shock than surprise surfaced. How in the hell's she counseling the son of the wanted drug lord that Maxwell was after? How the fuck did this happen? Yasmeen and Maxwell's eyes collided and all thirty pairs of eyes were on them.

There was silence as they tried to comprehend what is happening. Maxwell knew that she had worked with some of the officers on different cases so it wasn't them that was in shock, just her and him.

"Yasmeen?" Lieutenant Bailey broke their connection and continued. "Why don't you come to see me and tell me what you can? Meeting dismissed." He waved his hand to the officers in the room.

In minutes, they all left including him. He didn't see her until a few hours later she entered his office with a beautiful smile on her face to say "hi" after she met with Lieutenant Bailey. Before she could say anything else, he told her that he was going to question the kid. Then words were exchanged. Maxwell felt a presence in his office and raised his head from his hands to see Lieutenant Bailey shaking his head.

"You gonna have to leave this alone, Halifax until she says it's okay," Lieutenant Bailey told Maxwell.

"I do?" Maxwell asked raising an eyebrow.

"Yes. You've to move out. I know you two have been living together. You still have a chance to get Fernando," the Lieutenant informed him.

"I do." Maxwell now rises on his feet and looks at the Lieutenant.

"Yes, what she's doing is not so bad. She really doesn't know anything as yet, she will soon. She had this kid Izzy, counseling him for about three to four months now and he never told her anything. If he did, I would have known."

"What?" Maxwell said in shock as his face turned pink then red.

"Yes, she tells me whatever the client tells her about an illegal activity and the clients know she does because for her to live here she is honest and straight with everyone. We protect her as much as we can. She can walk the street because the juveniles protect her also."

"You two are good friends?"

"Friends no, working colleagues, yes. We have an understanding."

"I see."

"I hope you do Halifax, she saved a few of the officers' lives when someone put a hit out on them. She knows before we do. The men respect her. They have a soft spot for her." Maxwell understood. He realized who would not love his Meena, his Meena. What a mess he made of things, saying those horrible things to her.

"You know, Halifax, this would put a test on how strong both of your love is for each other. Your girl has integrity."

"Thanks," Maxwell said to the Lieutenant's shoulders as he left his office and closed the door. He picked his car keys up and dialed his work partner's cell phone number. He took the stairs while leaving a message on the phone. He has to collect some things and find a place to stay until this case blows over. How long he doesn't know except he cannot share the same address any longer with her. He called his father as he pulled out onto the main road heading to their apartment. His dad answered his call and he explained the whole conversation, bringing him up to date.

"Dad, I don't get it."

"She's doing her job and you are doing yours." His dad told his son. "It happens to be on the same side of the spectrum however you are having the mmmm different perception."

"That I know. Why?" Maxwell asked. He is desperate to understand this new development in his behavior.

"You were taught to protect and serve and Yasmeen doesn't need that. All she wants is your love. That's good enough for her. Some women need more, she doesn't," Darren concluded.

"Oh, I got it. What scares me is how dangerous this case is and she's caught upright in the middle of it. One move on her side and there can be a hit on her. If she let me talk to the kid, we get what we want and we move on, taking her away from the mess of the whole affair."

"Yes. She doesn't need you to save her, son. She can do that for herself. It's the easy way out son. What about that innocent child. Doesn't he have a right to live a free life like you and Yasmeen?"

"Yep, he does, dad. I got her point on that and yours too, thanks." He gulped his anger inward and then a thought he had stored during Lieutenant Bailey's chat now popped up.

"Oh, Dad! One more thing, can you and Mom buy the land for us to build our house for me and Meena until we get this case behind us."

"Are you sure you want to do that?"

"Yes, we looked for this land for a long time and we both wanted it. We have an architect's blueprint of our dream house. You have access to my account so I will send you all the authorization and contact numbers. It's a go." Maxwell had his will written and his parents had access to his account due to his travels and job. He had never changed it although he now wants to leave it all to Yasmeen if anything ever happened to him. He made a mental note to speak to the lawyer about it.

"Are you sure you two would be together after this?" His father asked.

"Yes, dad, I have faith in our love and I know this is the real emotion and our love will survive this conflict."

"Son, I had to ask. Your mom and I will be happy to buy the land and oversee the building of the house for you both. I'll have your mom call Yasmeen and have a chat with her and let her know what we are doing."

"Thanks, dad, she will appreciate it, I know she will."

"Bye, son."

"Bye, dad."

Daren put the telephone on the rack and went in search of his wife. He found her in the garden sitting on the swing reading a book. Her favorite mystery author and she looked as sexy as the day he married her. She looked up and smiled at him. She patted the seat next to her.

"Which one of our kids is it?"

"Maxwell and Yasmeen," he informed her.

"Oh no, what happened?" Darren filled her in and she nodded to the question of calling Yasmeen. She pulled herself off from her backside and stood her full length putting a hand out to her husband. He took it and they both walked back, hand in hand into the house. Abby dialed the number and left a message on Yasmeen's cellular phone.

Yasmeen was in a meeting with parents who are concerned about their daughter and could not answer when Abby called. Soon after the parents left, she spent the rest of the evening typing up notes and reports. It was after she arrived home that she saw the light on her cell phone, letting her know she had a message.

She put Jupiter on his lease and took him for a walk as she dialed into her voice mail. After several messages, she heard Abby's familiar voice. Maxwell had called them and she felt loved knowing his parents care about her. She hit the redial button and was happy to hear Darren's warm voice.

"I know this is hard for both of you. We're here not just for Maxwell for you too when either of you wanted to talk. We love you both very much."

"Thank you, Dad."

"You are welcome and now here's Abby."

"Hello dear, oh, my heart goes out to you both."

"Next time this happens I am giving the case to a colleague of mine. I refuse to work on the same case as Maxwell," Yasmeen informed her in a high sad voice.

"That's a good idea. Maxwell asked us to buy the land to build the house you two wanted. We are going to do it."

"Your son has faith in our love. That makes me feel very special to know that he believes in us. All the money Maxwell and I have saved is in an account. Let him manage the land and house with you. We have that worked out, already."

"Yes, that's our son." Abby beamed with a smile that Yasmeen felt. "Will do, love."

"Can I call you in a few days? I, I am taking Jupiter for a walk and don't feel like talking much."

"Of course, darling. Call us anytime and don't worry whatever you say stays between us."

"Thanks, Mum."

Yasmeen took a deep breath and turned around. Jupiter did not want to go home yet. He just got her and told her so that he will take his darn good time. Yasmeen gave him the attention he demanded and he she better not argue. She saw the note on the breakfast table the minute she let Jupiter off his lease. She picked it up and read it, not before her stomach contracted with a spasm of painful feelings. She knew it was from Maxwell.

"We have to live apart until the case is closed. I collected some things and will be staying over at the old place. No matter what, "I love you" Maxwell. Yasmeen's knees buckled after reading the note and she collapsed on the carpet, crying quietly at first then so loudly, Jupiter became scared. He ran to her and started to bark. She ignored him for a while and since his bark was in her ear, she picked him up and took him to bed with her. They both cuddled.

Jupiter was the happiest puppy ever. Tonight, he can sleep all night in the bed without being kicked off. He saw his other boss pack a bag and after giving him a walk, left. He's probably gone on a trip and will be back, therefore he is making the most of it. Jupiter and Yasmeen fell asleep exhausted from the day's event. There was not any familiar dream for either of them. Just as well.

There was merriment in the air, Anil's hand rested alongside the chair behind Yasmeen's shoulders. His face turned to hers laughing into her face with tears in his eyes. James and Rajput were looking at her laughing as well. Renée shook her head laughing with tears streaming down her face spoke. "That was the best sex joke I've heard," raising her Black and Tan to her lips.

Yasmeen was having dinner at the British pub with some of her friends. Anil and Rajput are partners living in Orange County. James is divorced with a son, Liam. Renee single, a probation officer had worked on a few cases with Yasmeen.

What she didn't know was that Maxwell would be here. She was well into her dessert of toffee rice pudding when she looked up and saw him looking at her with a questionable frown. His beautiful grey eyes were dark grey, intense with pain and longing.

A bit of jealousy gripped Maxwell's chest as his right hand lightly touched the spot of his ribcage. He felt lost without her and he wanted so desperately to walk over there, pull her out of his chair and kiss her until she melted in his arms. He had orders to leave her alone after their last meeting. He had to let things go her way until she feels it is safe.

It's her case and until she gave him the information needed to close his case, he cannot see her or contact her. Unless he can get the information, somewhere else, the last five years are over, and sending the drug lord to prison is also over. So many deaths of officers and innocent people, nonetheless fear and anger surfaced.

Maxwell can tell her that Ian had his eyes on Peter DaCosta for a long while however, he is in the clear. He wanted to ask her how Peter supported himself. He knew she does not send him money and he also knew that they have spoken often and e-mailed each other every day.

Yasmeen had mentioned her childhood friends, Peter DaCosta and Li Chang who live in Costa Rica to him after meeting his friends in Montana. Li Chang, she knew from photography class as he was the instructor. They had stayed in touch when he moved to Costa Rica to write a book on photography. He was on their list to visit in the near future.

Of all the luck, he has in his life, he had to fall in love with the one female who is involved in the same case as he does. What rotten luck, karma? He wondered. Love is not right; it seems that it is the one thing that never goes the way he wanted.

Well, he has never been around long enough to be in a serious relationship. He never met a strong lady before either. He has never been this happy and so miserable at the same time.

Love is right. It has been long lonely horrible weeks since he last held her. How he loved waking up next to her in the morning, making love to her in the early hours, how he missed her flirting, her touching, her kissing, and her looking at him trembling with joy. The little things he has gotten used to in a relationship. No one ever looked at him like that!

This is torture watching her laughing with her friends, hoping she missed him as much as he missed her. He saw her walking into the office building, talking to Lieutenant Bailey. He knows that because the Lieutenant always kept him informed of their visit or any new development in the case. He saw her in court a few times, not that he was keeping tabs on her.

Oh, no he trusted her with his life and he knew she trusted him with hers. It was merely how their paths crossed in different cases they are working on, in a different justice department.

He watched her gather her things and walk to the door of the pub. She stopped and waved at him, turning to her friends and whispering something. Next, he watched in horror, yet pleasant, as she strode toward him and planted a kiss on his opened mouth, smiled at his friends, and walked through the opened door.

"She loves you mon," "she is letting you know it's not over," "she is following protocol just like you," "she is telling you that she forgives you for the argument," his workmates were all saying at the same time to him. Maxwell slowly looked at all of his buddies, "Thanks."

His heart is beating faster than ever. He breathed in her scent of "afternoon delight" he had bought for her. He is happy that he was sitting and the table was hiding his arousal. He is in for a long, long lonely dreamless night, again, so what's new!

Yasmeen woke up moistened from another dream of making love. This time Maxwell was holding her in handcuffs to the cell, where and at what holding cell is a mystery to her. She tossed the bed covers off and her t-shirt, throwing it to join the covers somewhere by her feet where Jupiter lay. She held her pillow against her breast and tried to recapture the dream. Blurred and vague she had to think hard. They were both naked, with her legs wrapped around his hips.

Where? It's somewhere, where there were bars, not a cell at a police station, a gym probably nonetheless there was a place with bars because he carried her to the bars. Maxwell held her backside with his hands, kissing her as he walked. He was in her, locked down tight and secure.

Yasmeen's tongue darted out of her mouth and wet her red-hot lips. Then she gave her lover a love bite as he pushed all of him into her. Each time he pushed into her she made more music that came deep from within, sounds of music that only Maxwell can bring forth from her.

She remembered his hands came and removed her hand from his neck as he lifted her hands onto the bars. She tightly gripped them becoming more aroused than ever. She was dripping and ready as he tightened his muscles in her.

She yelled out his name asking for more, no she was begging for more. She smiled as she remembered she answered him in return as she contracted her muscles automatically. He tugged at her hair, giving her erected nipples a graze with his teeth, sending her into bliss beyond her wildest dream. He held her as she regained her breath; her hand left the bars as she clung to him.

He was still in her fully erected himself, kissing her eyes, down her cheeks to the hollow of her neck. He lingered there as she began to breathe slowly and gained control of herself. He moved deliberately slow, as he moved in and out of her.

Yasmeen's hands reached for the bars again and he pulled himself out from her. She shocked her head in a motion of protest. The sound died on her lips as he covered hers in a long passionate unforgettable kiss. His mouth moved down to her chin, down to the right nipple, and then to the next, tasting her soft brown skin, down to her stomach then down to her core of beauty. He took her in with his tongue as if it was medicine and he had the flu, only this bug is what he wanted, he welcomed.

"So, do I," She whispered as she felt him. It was nourishment for her, to have someone love her, as he never loved anyone in his life. She felt alive and vibrant, full of energy. In her dream, she sang a song out loud. She remembered she whispered his name so softly and she did now, "Maxwell." She began to cultivate herself.

As her hand reached her hot zone she can feel her lover's hands in her, she returned to her dream.

Maxwell moved his lips to the centerfold of her ladyhood as his fingers entered her, touching another centerfold of her hot spot, the g-zone. His tongue made magic while his fingers found her core. He began to release her secret cargo, slowly one stroke at a time. He found a rhythm as his fingers probed further in, stroked lazily in and out with the tip of his tongue lightly touching the inner sanctum of her ladyhood with a circular motion and sometimes zigzag moments. He kissed her lips.

She screamed louder and louder with music that came from within her. The melody filled the room and her lover began to feel the essence of the ride. He moved back and filled himself with her. He pulled back again and pushed deep into her as he lifted her legs onto his shoulders.

She was still holding on to the bars. She screamed again and found his rhythm. This was the breath of wildfire burning deep and rising high above the clouds, which sat on the frozen mountains peaks creating an avalanche of warmth meshed together that will melt any ozone.

As Maxwell picked up speed, he watched her tongue run over her lips and he contracted in her. She made a sound from deep within; very deep within as she returned the favor and contracted, he plunged deep and faster into her. His eyes connected with hers for a brief moment as she pushed her head back and screamed his name over and over again, until she let go of the bars and subsided loose onto him, her legs crippled besides his thighs.

He held her and slowly sank both of them to the cold tiled floor. They held each other until they catch their breath and gained control of the present moment.

"Maxwell." She bought herself to a climax. Maxwell laid awake thinking of the times his lover whispered his name. How he missed her! His heart is broken and he feels so alone.

"Yasmeen, I love you, oh, how I love you." Her name was a whispering breeze on his lips.

10

Three months later, Yasmeen slipped an address under Maxwell's office door. She told Lieutenant Bailey where the drugs were hidden and he wrote it down on a paper so Yasmeen can be left out of it. This is the paper that she slipped under his door. Anyone who wants to trace the note and handwriting will lead back to the Lieutenant.

Izzy Del Fernando was beginning to talk and he was confident that his dad would not figure it was him ratting on him. Yasmeen had shown him copies of the photograph Maxwell had of his father and different men. They had decided to say this is what made the connection.

Lieutenant Bailey briefed Yasmeen on how to protect herself as well as Izzy. After Adrian, Del Fernando is put away for life, everyone involved in this case will be able to live a safe life. He now nodded at Yasmeen as she turned and waved goodbye, mouthing the word. "Thank you."

All heads in the office turned and looked at her back as she took the stairs down to where her car was parked. They feel for both her and Maxwell. They know of his relationship with Yasmeen however they cannot be involved. They had told both of them, separately that they supported them.

"Get back to work, ladies, the show is over," the Lieutenant said loudly as all eyes returned to the task in front of them. The night was a long one as Yasmeen waited in bed with Jupiter for the call from Lieutenant Bailey on the raid of the warehouse in Casselberry. She was stroking Jupiter and on the brink of falling asleep when the call came sometime after two in the morning.

"It's a hit." Roared the Lieutenant and the phone went dead, the joy ringing in his voice.

"Halifax, your work has paid off. This jerk is going down for life. His fingerprint is all over this product. Guess he didn't didn't figure we'll find his stash. Good work boys, let's go home to our wives and children."

The lieutenant turned around and looked at Maxwell's saddened expression. "Sorry, I didn't mean...."

"It's okay," Maxwell reassured him. "We'll be together soon and I will never work on the same case as Yasmeen. I will give it to another officer."

"That's a smart choice, Halifax."

Maxwell walked toward his group of DEA agents as they drove to the office for debriefing and paperwork. It would be a long night. No one will be going home until the captain gave the clear message that all is done after the debriefing. Every single piece of evidence has to be bagged, tagged, and photographed.

All paperwork will be in order and nothing will be left for later. He heard Lieutenant Bailey make a call and knew it was to Yasmeen. She pulled through for him after all. Her way was safer, much safer he acknowledged. This was a valuable lesson he'd learned. It made his love for her deeper and their relationship stronger.

The evidence was against Adrian Del Fernando and he was not allowed to post bail. The trial will be next however Maxwell can go home now that there is a case against Del Fernando. There is no longer any danger that the evidence has been tampered with or cannot be used against the drug lord. It took another four months before the case went to court due to the compelling evidence against Del Fernando.

The drug lord who once roamed the high seas of the Caribbean was sentenced to life in prison without parole. It was a victory for everyone, a long-awaited victory for all the law enforcement officers involved, more for Adrian Del Fernando's wife and son, Izzy. They came forward and told what they knew, more on the disguises and where they lived. This sealed the life sentence on Del Fernando.

Yasmeen and Maxwell had missed their second anniversary due to the months of separation. Yasmeen didn't attend the trial nor did she testify. Her name was never mentioned as she closed the case of Izzy before giving

Lieutenant Bailey the address of Izzy's father Adrian Del Fernando's warehouse.

Detective Ian Blackwood flew in from Barbados and testified. Charges were filed against Del Fernando in Barbados. Officer Fred Millard also flew in from St. Lucia and testified against Del Fernando. There are charges filed against him and a warrant out for his arrest in other countries.

The couple flew in from England verifying the photographs. If by some miracle, Del Fernando gets out of prison, Barbados and St. Lucia prison await him. American prisons are spas compared to Caribbean prisons, therefore, he'll die there.

Maxwell drove home to Yasmeen and found Jupiter. He was jumbling up and barking as he was happy to see his master. He missed him terribly and he cannot understand why he was away for so long. Jupiter is not complaining either as he had Yasmeen all to himself. He was cuddling with her every night!

"I thought you didn't want to see me here as you get to sleep in the bed all night. Don't worry; we have a king-size bed so you're gonna have your own space." Maxwell informed Jupiter of the coming events. He dialed his parents' telephone number and told them the good news that the case is all over.

The minute he closed his phone he heard the door being opened. Yasmeen walked in and stood staring at him. They were not supposed to be together unless.....

"The case is closed." Maxwell stepped closer and relieved her with the bag of groceries. He turned back to her, pulled her out of the door toward him, and closed the door. He turned the lock. Yasmeen felt the impact of Maxwell's chest against her breast and did not care. They were free, free to be together. They both had lost sleep and weight in the last nine months they had lived apart. She wrapped her arms around his waist as Maxwell pulled her down on the carpet floor.

They held on to each other for a very long time, with Maxwell occasionally rubbing her skin and kissing her. They moved to the bed and lay there nourishing each other, enjoying and cherishing the moment. She lifted her lips and received the energy of his love.

Jupiter lay at their feet and put his hands over his eyes. He knows what's coming next and no more bed for him. Oh, well he sighed now his mistress will not cry anymore. Both his master and mistress are together and he will be spoiled like before, what more can a puppy ask for?

Maxwell remembered he wanted to know about Peter. He voiced the question: "How does your friend Peter support himself?"

"He helped me through counseling school to get my doctorate. It was a lot more than my parents planned and I didn't want to ask them for any money. They did so much for me already, I asked Peter. I paid him back with the rent from the beach house I inherited. He takes care of it for me. He also made some investment in the stock market before the depression and it paid off beautifully. Why do you ask?"

Maxwell told her about Ian and his investigation. He told her he couldn't tell her. She understood and sat up and looked at her lover.

"Let us negotiate now. We will not work on any case, the other is involved in."

Maxwell sealed the deal with a kiss, pulling her to lie on the pillow. He pulled his Meena on top of him. They touched and cuddled until both fell asleep. This silence was a nourishing one, a silence so golden it spilled into days of pure pleasure of nurturing the essence of each other.

A few days later, they were packing things into boxes. Maxwell playfully smacked his Meena on her backside. She grinned at him and blew him a kiss. He caught it. What began as a tease ended in something loving. He was caught unaware by the passion that arose in him. Then he walked over and she ran from him, laughing.

The passion now engulfed him and he was on a mission

with no intention of losing. He gave chase and caught her in a few seconds of his commencing. His hand went around her waist and the other was lost in her hair. She avoided his kiss and went for his neck, giving love bites as she worked her way down. She gripped hold of his t-shirt with her teeth and pulled it up to his mouth. He took it from her, their eyes made contact.

They clung tighter as they allowed the absorption of sensations to float through them. They let it build to a high degree of passion until they cannot stand it any longer. Pure passion of bliss overtook them to ride the waves of paradise. They began to undress each other, kissing and touching throughout the journey of making love. He pulled her onto the carpet floor, the weight of his body now almost covering hers, their hands moving eagerly as though they couldn't touch enough of each other.

Maxwell didn't wait to fill himself in her. She welcomed the intrusion of him in her as she felt her body absorb every inch of him. The intense physical pleasure of his possession awakened her core with pure delight, giving way to the wakeful nights they had spent away from each other. Those months seem a memory now, as they lay there, holding and devouring each other.

It was swift and urgent and gentle with an abundance of love with the sweetness of tantalizing of tingled sensations. They looked into each other's eyes filled with the energy of pure joy of love. This love had broken the bond of frozen hearts, only to deliver true love. They got it and they understood how precious it is for them to have received this gift. They treasured every moment.

Yasmeen pulled Maxwell's head and puckered a kiss so passionate that his muscles jerked in her and she contracted her muscles. He pushed into her and as she loosened her hold on his lips she whispered, "I love you, Maxwell Liam Halifax." He pulled out a little and drove right into her as if he was a wild fire breathing on a hot scorching day. They picked up a rhythm, sending them both into a spiral of new musical notes.

"I love you." He whispered in her ear, releasing all of him into her, filling her as if he never did before and she welcomed all of him. They lay there in the aftermath of their lovemaking touching each other and smiling, only to be disturbed by the rustling of paper by their feet.

Jupiter had dived into the box with groceries that were for dinner, feasting on the tuna, which was no longer wrapped in paper. It was the last lot of food in the refrigerator as the kitchen utensils were all packed in boxes ready to be moved into the new house.

"I guess we have a lot of cleaning up to do." Yasmeen looked lovingly at Maxwell. "And we're eating out."

The next big move was into the new house. Maxwell was on a well-deserved vacation, while Yasmeen hired another counselor, Dr. Petra Garcia who would fill in for her as well as work on Mondays and Fridays. Yasmeen now works Tuesdays to Thursdays, starting at nine in the morning until eight at night.

Yasmeen and Maxwell had decided to donate money to a world organization that gave aid to disadvantaged men, women, and children. They chose to support the organization that fought to supply everyone with drinking water. Daren and Abby joined forces with them and before they knew it they had a charity organization.

When family, friends, and colleagues heard about it they too began donating money. They planned to become active in the organization as well as visit the countries and meet the people. The house was completed and they were ready to be moved in. Trees were planted all around for privacy; they were planning a kitchen and flower garden. New furniture was delivered and whatever time they had left after the day's work, they curled up together exhausted.

Almost everything was packed and ready for the final move. Yasmeen put her apartment up for sale and had a few prospective buyers. Maxwell's boxes from the basement were shipped to the new house. Darren and Abby want to be there to give a helping hand as they move into their new home, however, the overseeing of building the house took a toll on them and a vacation was desperately needed. They are off with friends to Malta. Peter came from Barbados to give them a hand with the final move. He is off to California to visit a girlfriend then sailing with some buddies. He promised to visit more often and look forward to their visit to Barbados. Yasmeen had decided as soon as she repaid Peter the money she owed him she would not be renting her beach home or only temporarily renting it. A weekend getaway would do them some good when their work becomes stressful.

Today, however, Yasmeen was stuck at the office counseling. Jupiter was at her heels, smelling, and sniffing. Maxwell and his workmates were putting the finishing touches of paint to the last room as the beds were due to arrive tomorrow. The master room was decorated and the king-size bed was in place. They can sleep in their new home tonight.

One of the three rooms would be used as an office, the other as a movie room, and the last one for a guest room. The office and the movie room can be turned into a bedroom when all of Maxwell's family visited for Thanksgiving later this year.

The telephone in the office rang and Yasmeen jumped. Her assistant, Li Ann answered it. Yasmeen walked from the conference room to Li Ann's desk. She was told that her last appointment was canceled for next week. At the same time, her present one just arrived.

Several hours later, Yasmeen pulled up at their new home. Maxwell heard Jupiter barking and left the office where he was putting his desk together to greet her. She saw him coming to her and stopped in her tracks. She held her breath. Maxwell was shirtless and in shorts with a slight tan. She couldn't move. She felt moistened and she wanted him right there, NOW!

Maxwell saw her expression and grinned. He does not feel sexy, however, something on him turned his Meena on and that was good enough for him. A plan for tonight blew in his thoughts, these thoughts he welcomed. The forthcoming plans brew in his eyes and convey the hidden message to Yasmeen. Bright pink outlined her cheeks.

"I love it when you blush when I make you blush."

The color on her cheeks became pinker. Maxwell took the packages

of food from her and gave her a deep long kiss, sending her knees weak. He held her with one hand and stood looking at her speechless blushed face. A very wicked grin touched his eyes.

"We could go behind de bushes and have wild sex." He informed her. Yasmeen's blush deepened, she was still speechless. He looked at her still grinning. He leaned closer and whispered in her ear.

"Deep breath, my love, deep breath and forget the wild sex. I will make love to you slowly tonight. We have to christen the bed. We have to go into the house, the boys are waiting." He told her as they walked into the open front door. The atmosphere was heavy with the smell of fresh paint. The boys were all standing in the kitchen having beers awaiting the food Yasmeen picked up from the Chinese restaurant. They noticed Yasmeen's blush cheeks.

"What took you so long? We thought we'd to come and look for you in the bushes," Officer Peterson said.

Yasmeen smiled and said nothing. She moved to take the food out of the bag and display it for all to help themselves. She walked outside pretending to look around the garden, Jupiter on her heels.

Really, she needed a breather. Too much testosterone in there and all they are going to do is tease her. Let them tease Maxwell, he can take it. Besides she knows he does the same to the other officers, male bonding.

"We don't do quickies. You are all leaving real early, today. We will move the rest tomorrow. Thank you, gentleman. After you eat you may kindly leave and go home to your lovers." Laughter filled the air. Yasmeen heard him blush beet red with a secret smile on her lips.

Several weeks into the moving, Maxwell dove into the pool and swam to one side then to the next. Perfect he thought thought as he walked out of the pool onto the lawn. He looked around over the deck where the grill stood, then to the back surveying the hedges, and then to the other side. He was pleased that the hedges blocked all visibility outward, therefore no one can see inward unless they are pushing the hedges aside to look. They had privacy therefore they can play all they want in the backyard.

Maxwell grinned that wicked smile as he dove again into the pool. He needs to keep in shape as Yasmeen is into yoga and Thi Chi class. The house was built to suit them and it sat on an acre of land. An FBI, Federal Bureau of Investigation agent is building his house on one side and a police officer on the other side. Yasmeen wanted security and she got it. Well, maybe not that type of security she meant, so what?

Yasmeen has his security and safety as well from the neighbors. Funny, how he felt insecure with her love, and all along she was feeling insecure with his love. They need the same assurance all along. How many misconceptions did they have of each other and their relationship?

Glad that the rocky road is now paved with pure love for each other and it is as secure as it can ever be for them. The lake sits at the back with a spectacular view of the sun setting. Yasmeen sold her apartment to a newly wedded police officer and his wife. In a few weeks, her beach house in Barbados would be vacant.

Peter would see to it that it would be ready for them when he returned from his sailing trip. She is taking Maxwell there before they go to India for their fourth anniversary.

Maxwell's vacation would be up soon. At least he has another two weeks and will return to work after his parents visit them in two days. He opened his boxes, finally. He had forgotten what was in them. It would be fun returning to his past and sharing it with his Meena.

Lieutenant Bailey had one of the officers boxed his personal things from his office and Meena collected it. They all sit there waiting to be sorted. He now has his desk job and only works in Seminole County. No more traveling unless it is with Yasmeen on vacation. Life is great.

His parents would be here from Malta tomorrow for a week. All would be unpacked and the rest of the unwanted things would be given to a homeless shelter. They wanted to make the home warm and full of love by the time his parents arrive.

Abby had helped Yasmeen put a photo album together with her and Maxwell. They finished the quilt Abby had started for them as a home-warming gift. It matched the master room, which was painted in sky blue with silver trimmings. This was done while they were separated not so long ago.

Jupiter had his own basket with a quilt for the time he would accidentally be kicked off the bed. Although they have a king-size bed, Yasmeen had explained to Jupiter, Maxwell gets crazy, sometimes when he sleeps. Maxwell laughed as Jupiter bowed his head.

Two days later as the sun sets, father and son were grilling steak and fish with potatoes, broccoli, and drinking beer, Abby and Yasmeen joined them with plates and glasses of wine.

"Well, my young loves, how is dinner coming?" Abby looked lovingly at the pair, who now turned and give the ladies attention.

"We'll be done in about three minutes," Maxwell informed them as he put his arm around Yasmeen's waist and planted a quick kiss on her lips.

"In that case, your mother and I want to give you both a toast," Darren announced.

All bottles and glasses were raised as the senior Halifax spoke. "To the two most wonderful people who have beaten the odds in their relationship. We wish you both love and peace as Abby and I have in our partnership. We know your love will pull you both through the difficult times, as it has already proven and you both have many more loving years."

Yasmeen and Maxwell both said thank you at the same time while bottles and glasses touched with unity and love. After they drank, they hugged each other and had dinner under the Florida moon and stars.

This was Maxwell's last night home. His parents left this morning with a promise they would join them for a long weekend in the Smokey Mountain in Georgia.

Yasmeen heard a splash as she was preparing lunch for them.

them. She took two steps backward and saw Maxwell diving nude into the pool. She put the sandwiches into the refrigerators and ran into their bedroom. She pulled a drawer out and hurriedly took her clothes off. Maxwell had bought her this bikini set and she never wore it.

Guess today is a good day to christen it. It has been a while, two weeks since they made love. They couldn't, while his parents were here, though they were inventive with other nighttime entertainment. They were on alert and it was not as satisfying as when they are all alone. Soon they would be both back to work and too tired for much except on weekends providing Maxwell is not working.

They have the whole evening and night to make up for the lost time. Besides the pool needs christening and she will just have to make Maxwell spur his engine. It needs to be greased because when it is idling, it gets rusty and needs lots of work to be up and ready at the spur of the moment. We girls have to keep the engine greased and oiled she spoke out loud and laughed as Jupiter barked.

Thinking about how she will seduce him makes her full of warmth and she moistened. She was ready. He does this to her all the time. It gets worse when he looks at her with love and passion in his eyes. She melts and is speechless. Her knees began to buckle and Yasmeen took three consecutive breaths to regain enough strength to walk out to swim with her lover, well maybe not swim.

Yasmeen came out through the back door with a beer in one hand and a glass in the other. She lay both down next to the pool and walked down the stairs into the pool. She swam to Maxwell and held on to his shoulders, curling her legs over his waist. She looked into his eyes and saw the wicked grin he has when he is thinking about making love.

"What's it this time?" She asked, nipping on his lips. Her lips left his, tracing hungering down to the hollow of his neck, and quickly back up to his ear. Maxwell's engine was turned on and he stood tall. Yasmeen giggled as she felt him. She pumped up his jam a bit more as she nibbled on the loop of his ear and let her tongue lightly touch his inner nerves.

Maxwell needs no more encouragement as his hands pulled at the string of her bikini. His thumb and index finger plucked at the string of her bikini top, which led to her back and then at the back of her neck. In an instant, both were swimming away from them. Maxwell had nothing on, therefore; he had nothing to take off.

He kissed her gently at first, nipping at her lips, teasing her. In a moment of insanity, he brewed a passionate kiss so quickly that Yasmeen held her breath. He pulled her on top of him and swam on his back, taking them both under the water for a second or two before surfacing on solid ground. He stood tall above his waist, deep in water.

He claimed a stand and pulled her into him as her legs circled him again. He slipped his tongue farther into her mouth as he cupped her neck and held her lips to his, and then he entered her. Fiery sensations broke out in all parts of their bodies, joining their heart and breath as one. He withdrew and touched the tip of her tongue with his and he said, "Look, my love."

Her eyes left his and followed him. She looked as he cupped her backside, pulled her away from him, and then he did the unthinkable. He entered her again. They both lost control of their senses. He rocked deeper as Yasmeen arched her head and back away from him, making more melody for a new unfinished song.

He rocked deeper and his hips provoked hers. He nipped on her nipples as if he never tasted them before in his life. Her nails curved her trademarks along his lower back, sinking into his skin as she felt her body begin to rock to his rhythm. They both tightened their muscles at the same time and both quivered with delight.

She felt a massive surge of ecstasy taking over as lips touched, enveloping them. He sank deeper into her, pushing further, quicker and harder as his muscles tightened, his hand cupped her backside freezing her to him. His hips rocked against hers, they exploded as a fury of trade winds.

Epilogue

The stone pillars stand strong on the four corners of the pool. It was almost dusk in the very hot evening making the pillars gleam a ghostly light into the pool and over the grill. Long-running plants with bright red flowers sat on the pillars, giving a romantic touch to the area. The air was scented with roses and palm trees.

Sounds of music play an old familiar Indian love song, "Kabi Kabi." A song they had made love to many times. A year into settling in their home, Yasmeen e-mails Maxwell and invites him to a sexy evening. Jupiter had a mate of his own, Saturn, who was a five-anniversary present. The three of them visit an animal shelter and Jupiter chose her as his mate.

Finally, she has to explain to him about the fatal day he took her photograph and how he sealed their fate together. She had removed the framed photograph in one of the boxes she collected from the office. She had plans for it. If Maxwell had taken the photographs and let it go, it would have died off.

Instead, he became fascinated with her and a bit obsessed. He began daydreaming, which turned into wet dreams. To make matters worse, well not worse more intensified he applied his heart and even had her photograph framed, standing on his desk. Every day his energy generated a magnet towards her energy pulling them together.

How can you explain something like this to anyone? When Maxwell made a wish for the future, an unconscious wish of meeting a girl of his dreams, he made the dream with the passion of his heart by feeling and thinking about it. Then he began adding intense feelings into his thoughts, manifesting a sexual dream of them together, making his wish halfway made.

Maxwell had consciously framed her photograph adding his heart, which signified love into his wish, and before they knew it, they physically met and had fallen in love.

Actually, they were already in love before they met; they had no choice only to accept it as a fact. Would Maxwell understand the Law of Attraction? He's a very opened minded person and loved all cultures. He is not spiritual and pretty much thinks what she does is "cool." How would he take this? That the girl in the photograph and she are one and the same!

She was watching Jupiter and Saturn playing with an old chewed-up ball when Maxwell walked through the back door leading into the pool area. He was dressed in black slacks, a white shirt, a black tie with his gun on his left side, and his badge. He is so sexy!

She was in the pool in a blue-striped bikini when she saw him. She hurriedly climbed out and stopped him in his tracks.

"Wait right there. No, go back three steps and close your eyes.

"What?"

"Oh, just follow orders for once in your life."

The silence was golden as she hurriedly tied the blue and white wrap on her waist, the very one in the photograph. She walked toward him.

"You can open your eyes now."

Maxwell quickly opened his eyes and let out his breath. His face was rosy from the anticipation of what was in store for him. Now shock surfaced then surprise took over as he processed the image in front of him. He had recognized the blue and white batik wrap. He had seen it before and then his grey eyes gave way to memory.

Those days so long ago, he had taken a photograph of a girl wearing the same batik wrap. No, it can't be, yet it feels like it is, his Meena, is the girl in the photograph!

"No. It can't be, you are her!" He whispered in disbelief. This was too much as an overwhelming sensation taken over. He was speechless then a memory surfaced. He took a long deep breath fighting for control enough to voice his memory.

"I threw the photograph away. I wish I hadn't now." Sadness joined his overwhelmed emotions.

"No, my love you didn't. I removed it from your things in the box."

"You did?" It was all he would say.

"Yes, I had plans for it. It is lying by the table in our office."

"You knew when you came to the office the first time." Maxwell was still putting the pieces together. His heart pumped hard as his brains kept shifting into his memory and stayed in the present moment.

Yasmeen walked towards him with a wicked grin on her face. She pulled on his tie, drawing him to her lips. She wrapped her arms around his waist and hugged him, tight. He was shaking from shock and then electrifying sensations pumped into his heart.

Passion coupled with the energy of their love overcame him. His arms went around her wet body. He still could not believe it.

"You knew all this time." He put his forehead on hers breathing in deep, very deep.

"Yes, I wanted to plan how I was going to tell you, now is perfect."

She will explain later to him however for now she removed her arms from around his waist, rested her head on his chest for a few minutes listening to his heartbeats.

All went silent for a while, even Jupiter and Saturn who were looking at their master and mistress. They both knew what would happen next. Jupiter had told his life partner Saturn about his master and mistress so she is well informed about their behavior. She looked at Jupiter and he nodded his head in a silent agreement that noise is about to break the silence.

In zinc with Jupiter and Saturn, Yasmeen looked up at Maxwell and felt his arousal. She brushed his lips in teasing kisses. Foreplay had begun so long ago on the beach in Barbados where a gentleman saw his lady. There was no mistake as to what the next hours held for these two lovers.

Synchronicity had worked its magic and pulled through what the Laws of Attraction couldn't do alone. Together they made the unthinkable became a reality. One lonely DEA agent sending a wish to meet his mate and he received more than he asked for that day so long ago he took the photographs.

The counselor who felt lost in a world where there seems more pain than joy met someone who she understood and who understood her, who had the courage to believe in their love, and who gave her the security of his love. Call it what you want serendipity, synchronicity, or life, it can happen to provide the heart is evoked into playing a role.

Somewhere over the lake, hidden from their view, a whispering breeze blew the curtain over the table that holds a photograph of a girl clad in a blue striped bikini and a blue and white batik wrap.

A spoon with their photograph was placed next to the frame. A dried red and white rose gave the collaboration of true love. In the distance, a bird sang their song as the trade winds blew across the distant ocean.